PENGUIN BOOKS

WHY VOTE LAB

Tony Wright was born
his father worked at C   ...esborough
Primary School and to K   ...ool. He went on to
the London School of Econ   ...here he took a first-class degree;
Harvard University, as a Kennedy Scholar; and Balliol College,
Oxford. After lecturing at the University College of North Wales at
Bangor, he moved in 1975 to the University of Birmingham, to work
in adult education. He was Reader in Politics there in 1992, when he
won the Cannock and Burntwood seat for Labour in the general
election. Before his election he had been chair of South Birmingham
Community Health Council and active in the world of school
government.

He has written many books, pamphlets and articles. His most recent
books are *Citizens and Subjects* (1993) and *Socialisms: Old and New*
(1996), and he is a regular contributor to press, radio and television,
as well as co-editor of the *Political Quarterly*.

Tony Wright is married and has three sons. His recreations are
gardening, tennis, books and waiting for Wolverhampton Wanderers
to win promotion.

Why Vote Labour?

Tony Wright MP

PENGUIN BOOKS

PENGUIN BOOKS

Published by the Penguin Group
Penguin Books Ltd, 27 Wrights Lane, London W8 5TZ, England
Penguin Books USA Inc., 375 Hudson Street, New York, New York 10014, USA
Penguin Books Australia Ltd, Ringwood, Victoria, Australia
Penguin Books Canada Ltd, 10 Alcorn Avenue, Toronto, Ontario, Canada M4V 3B2
Penguin Books (NZ) Ltd, 182–190 Wairau Road, Auckland 10, New Zealand

Penguin Books Ltd, Registered Offices: Harmondsworth, Middlesex, England

First published 1997
10 9 8 7 6 5 4 3 2 1

Set in 10.5/13pt Monotype Sabon
Typeset by Rowland Phototypesetting Ltd, Bury St Edmunds, Suffolk
Printed in England by Clays Ltd, St Ives plc

Contents

Preface

I need to say a word about what follows. It is not a party manifesto, even a disguised one. The air will be thick with those and there would be little point in producing another. So there are none of those neat manifesto-like policy headings, because life is not really lived in such tidy segments and a general argument should try to weave in and out of them. Nor is it encumbered more than is absolutely necessary with all those figures that politicians like to use but which few understand and are often bogus anyway. A final disavowal is that what follows carries no official party seal of approval, and is my responsibility alone.

If that explains what this little book is not, I should also say what it is. It is one person's argument for voting Labour in this election, highly personal, sometimes polemical, written at a reckless speed, and as honest as I can make it. The person in question happens, for the moment, to be a politician, but if it reads like a politician's book then it has failed in its purpose. It explains why I shall be voting Labour. If its argument persuades anybody else, that will be a bonus.

Tony Wright

ONE

Ends and Beginnings

One evening last week a friend went to catch the 10.24 train from Victoria Station to his home in Croydon. As the station clock showed the time as 10.22, he was naturally dismayed when he saw the train departing from the platform. Remonstrating with a station official and calling in aid the evidence displayed by the clock, there came back this immortal reply: 'I am sorry, sir, but that is a Railtrack clock.' Just one incident of course, one more lunacy to add to the long list of lunacies and indignities that make up so many aspects of life in this country after nearly two decades of unbroken Conservative rule, but a pattern begins to emerge. It is of a country that is becoming a different place from what it once thought it was, its values and institutions subverted not from without but from within, and its people gloomily uncertain about both their own future and the future of their country.

A few months ago I received, along with other Members of Parliament, a circular letter from Severn Trent plc, one of the privatized water companies. One item in this letter particularly caught my attention. It reported that, since privatization, its customers had displayed a 'reluctance' to save water when the company had requested them to do so at times of water shortage. The company was obviously perplexed by this behaviour on the part of its customers, those Conservative politicians whose dogma required that this natural monopoly should be privatized might also be perplexed by it, but to everyone else such behaviour is the plainest common sense. It might be reprehensible, but it is entirely understandable. When the old bureaucratic water boards were in trouble, people might curse them but they were prepared to help out with their 'own' water. Now they think of shareholders and boardroom excesses and defiantly keep their hose-pipes on. Just one more incident of course, but replete with meaning for those in search of the larger pattern of our troubled times.

I am writing this on Budget Day. As expected, Chancellor Kenneth Clarke has just announced the cut in income tax that is designed to buy votes for the Conservative Party at the election. It is an unashamedly political calculation, made in defiance of the state of the public finances and the advice of his own experts. Yet even after this political penny off income tax, people are still paying much *more* tax than when the self-proclaimed tax-cutting Conservatives came to office (a post-Budget calculation by the Institute for Fiscal Studies showed that households would still be paying an average of nearly £400 a year more in tax than they would have done under the 1992 tax regime) and on the Government's own Budget figures the total tax burden is set to *rise* year on year (from 35.25 per cent of GDP this year to 38 per cent in five years' time). As income tax generates only just over a quarter of government revenue, playing with the basic rate has far more to do with political gimmickry than with the serious business of taxing and spending. Prudence required an attack on the debt ratio and a decision not to imperil long-term stability by overheating a recovering economy. Politics evidently required a symbolic tax cut, despite the evidence that most voters would prefer to safeguard public services (and one of the Chancellor's many sleights of hand was to pay for his income tax cut by loading it onto Council Tax). The Conservatives believe that a crude tax bribe won them the last general election and hope that it will not be remembered that this was immediately followed by a huge tax hike. They hope to perform the same trick again now. What they may have overlooked is the fact that people do not usually fall for the same bogus bargain twice.

This Budget was the Conservative Government's last card. It was supposed to be the dramatic trick that would restore its political fortunes as the election approached. That it has conspicuously not done so has less to do with the Budget itself, despite its transparently political conjuring, than with the country to which this final Conservative Budget was delivered. For this is also the country of the Railtrack clock and the lamentations of Severn Trent plc. If we extend our gaze for a moment from Budget Day to Budget Week, noticing just some of the reports from our own country during the brief space of a few November days, it soon becomes clear why a familiar trick is no longer able to work its traditional effects. I offer the following items, taken almost at random. I simply happened to notice them; no doubt others could have been chosen and would make the point equally well. Nor do I want to give any extended comment on them, for they tell their own story.

First there was this letter in the *Independent* from a doctor who clearly felt the need to describe the real-life consequences of the NHS internal market:

> Sir: I am unable to remain silent any longer about the hypocrisy of the Government's reassurances about the state of the National Health Service.
>
> I am a consultant anaesthetist working in a university teaching hospital. Part of my work consists of outpatient consultation and treatment for patients

with chronic pain. Budgetary constraints upon both purchaser and provider have led to a reduction in the number of patients my consultant colleague and I are able to treat. I have today been advised that henceforth I should prioritize new outpatient appointments according to whether the referral general practitioner is a fundholder, rather than solely on clinical criteria.

I do not seek to blame the Southampton University Hospitals NHS Management Trust for their advice. If the NHS is to be run on a competitive internal market basis such a policy is inevitable, and indeed we now have differential waiting lists for other medical specialities within the Trust based on the same criteria.

I challenge Stephen Dorrell and Gerald Malone (some of whose constituents are referred to me) to deny that this represents a two-tier system of medical care, based not upon the patient's ability to pay, but rather upon the GP's ability to pay. Patients have a right to know this.

DR DIANA BRIGHOUSE
Southampton

This is not a politician's voice, but a working doctor's, and is all the more telling because of it. It shows what running the NHS as a market, with different levels of service provided to those who can purchase most, means to those who work in it and those who depend upon it.

Then there was the shocking report of the national survey undertaken by the Health Visitors' Association, which revealed that diseases such as tuberculosis and rickets were again spreading among the poor. Nearly one third of health visitors found tuberculosis among the families they were involved with last year. It is not surprising that the headlines spoke of a return to Dickensian diseases in a country that had once believed social improvement had eradicated them for ever. Now they are back, at the end of the rich twentieth century, the product of the poor nutrition and bad social conditions that had spawned them in the last century. This survey coincided with another report, compiled from social security statistics by the House of Commons Library, which revealed that nearly one in three babies in Britain is now born into poverty. This is a return to Victorian values with a vengeance.

One consequence of this, as in Victorian times, is crime. Here another report in the same week put a stick of dynamite under the Conservative claim to be tackling the problem of law and order. It was a report on juvenile crime (*Misspent Youth: Young People and Crime*) from the Government's own Audit Commission. Its verdict could not have been more emphatic or damning. Despite the fact that over a quarter of known offenders are under 18 and youth crime costs us over a billion pounds a year, the Audit Commission discovered that: 'Overall, less is done now than a decade ago to address offending by young people.' The political rhetoric of law and order meets a policy reality of wasteful ineffectiveness: 'The current system for dealing with youth crime is inefficient and expensive, while little is being done to deal effectively with juvenile justice.' Yet, as this report also shows, there is much that could be done to prevent and deal with offending behaviour if there was the will and the imagination to do so. The fact that this is the verdict not of soft-hearted reformers but of hard-nosed auditors makes the indictment of Conservative failure in this area even more devastating. Talking tough while acting ineffectually soon becomes a pathetic spectacle.

I offer one further piece of evidence, not a report but a spillage. A letter from Michael Heseltine as Deputy Prime Minister to other ministers found its way into the newspapers. It described the difficulties the Government was having in 'selling' its approach to public services and proposed setting up 'panels of people associated with the public services who could be vigorous and attractive proponents of our policies'. This attempt to recruit cheerleaders for Conservative policies from within the public services was only thwarted when Sir Robin Butler, as Head of the Civil Service, took the view that this political recruitment task was an inappropriate role for civil servants to undertake. Yet what is extraordinary is that the Government should have considered that this *was* a permissible civil service function. If final evidence was needed of the perils of having one party in office for too long, this surely provides it.

These examples, plucked from a single week, tell us something about the kind of country we are becoming. They also tell us why a penny off the basic rate of income tax, or an economy put into buoyant pre-election mode, does not work its political magic any more. A Health Service fragmenting, banished diseases returning, child poverty intensifying, crime policy failing, ministers doing what ministers should not do: all this, and more (including the total failure of the London Underground system, a dramatic symbol of its chronic under-investment, on one evening during Budget Week), defines the real context in which this coming election is being fought. The choice now is whether we want to continue on the same path, with these kinds of consequence, or whether we want to strike out on a different route. There is no longer any excuse for not knowing what is at stake.

In what follows I want to consider what seem to me to be the key choices. Because we need to understand how we came to arrive at where we now are, I begin (Chapter Two) by comparing the prospectus offered by the 'new' Conservatives who took over their party and the country in 1979 with the bitter fruits of that prospectus now. I then discuss (Chapter Three) the renewal and transformation of the Labour Party – the making of New Labour under Tony Blair – that has brought hope to all those who want a sensible and radical party of reform to vote for and who understand that being sensible and being radical do not have to be alternatives. This leads on (Chapter Four) to a discussion of what I believe are the fundamental differences of values and beliefs between Labour and the Conservatives, on which a choice now has to be made that will shape the direction of this country for years to come. If we make the right choice, I argue (Chapter Five) that the basis exists for a new radical consensus in Britain that not only buries some old and unhelpful divisions but also offers the prospect of sustained policy initiatives on a range of important fronts. One of these fronts is the economy (Chapter Six), where Labour's stakeholding approach contrasts with the very different approach of the Conservatives and, even more importantly, opens up the possibility of the kind of sustained partnership that has been so elusive in the past. But we also have to decide whether we want to be a decent and responsible society (Chapter Seven), that includes all its citizens as members of one community, for this is an inescapable choice from which much else follows. Then there is the crucial issue of political reform (Chapter Eight), where Labour's programme for renewing and modernizing our democracy is opposed by a Conservative Party which refuses to accept or understand that the moment for reform has arrived. This election will also decide whether we want to become an effective player in Europe and the wider world (Chapter Nine), making a distinctive contribution to the partnerships for peace, security and justice, or whether we are content to remain in the state of introverted neurosis to which the warring condition of the Conservative Party has for so long consigned us. Finally, and most fundamentally, I suggest (Chapter Ten) that this election could be the moment when we decide what kind of society we would like to be and express this in a new civic vision.

This vision needs to be an honest vision. People have had enough of politicians who promise what they cannot deliver. Labour's 'early pledges' made last year showed the party's priorities – a windfall tax on the privatized utilities to fund schemes to get young people into work, putting the money saved from the Assisted Places Scheme into reducing class sizes in primary schools, switching NHS resources from bureaucracy to bringing waiting times down – but they also showed where the money was coming from to pay for them. The same approach informs all the pledges that Labour is making in this election. That is what a new and more honest politics demands – and what I believe people want. This election is not just about whether we get a new government, but also about whether we get a new kind of politics in Britain. As we near the end of a period of Conservative rule that stretches right back to 1979, we also approach the beginning of a new era in British politics. It is a good moment to recall the words spoken by Labour's former leader, John Smith, on the evening before he died: 'A chance to serve – that is all we ask.'

TWO

The Great Betrayal

'We just can't go on like this'
'I feel completely let down by them'
'They've had it as far as I'm concerned'

Hardly a day passes without someone in my Midlands constituency saying something of this kind to me. The pollsters and pundits report that the same phrases are being heard up and down the land. They suggest a fixed and deeply felt judgement, the product not of passing disenchantments but of lived experiences over these many years of Conservative rule. This no doubt explains why the familiar tactics of a Conservative Government about to face the electorate (a tax bribe here, a bout of foreigner-bashing there), even when combined with some of the most distasteful and disreputable propaganda techniques ever seen in this country, fail to elicit the once familiar response. The old buttons are pressed with ever more desperation, but the old reactions no longer come. Some Conservatives find this deeply puzzling; but others know that the game is up. People have been there, done that. They have had enough. And they want a change.

People know it is a tough old world out there, and getting tougher. They do, after all, live in it. They rightly distrust glib politicians claiming unique possession of a magic box.

But they also need to feel that they at least have a government which is on their side, not one which seems to be waging some kind of ideological war on them. I think of the proud elderly lady who came to see me recently, producing from her handbag a piece of paper on which she had carefully itemized all her essential outgoings against her meagre income, as she showed me the water bill that she had no means of paying. Other stories tell of other experiences. The family whose home was repossessed. The businessman who was wiped out by the recession. The youngsters desperate for a decent job. The middle-aged man who doubts if he will ever work again. The once pleasant estate now made a daily hell by crime, vandalism and drugs. The elderly couple, their pension eroded, who worry about what will happen to them and their house when they can no longer fend for themselves.

What all such experiences have in common is a pervasive sense of insecurity. While the Conservatives are celebrating the virtues of 'flexibility' and 'deregulation', it feels very different at the receiving end. Perhaps they do not know, or care, about the receiving end. If you are on a crazed ideological trip, you tend not to notice the casualties along the way. Yet the truth is that if this society becomes a more anguished and unpleasant place in which to live, then we are all casualties. And that is the big truth, sensed by more and more people, which goes behind and beyond the particular dissatisfactions and discontents that can readily be assembled. It is also what this election is really all about. It is about whether we want to be a more dynamic, more decent and more democratic society than we now are. Those who say we have to choose between economic dynamism and social decency are wrong, both empirically and morally, and when they say it with such obvious ideological glee they are damnably wrong. We badly need to become more successful economically in an intensely competitive world; but we need to be more successful socially too. And far from being alternatives, a strong economy and a strong society march hand in hand. That is the real lesson from those Asian 'tiger' economies about which so much nonsense is constantly spoken, although it is hardly necessary to journey so far in order to discover such an obvious and elementary home truth.

It is scarcely surprising that so many people (especially those who once trusted them and voted for them) describe their feelings about the Conservatives in terms of betrayal; for betrayal is what it is. A promise was made to the British people and that promise has been broken. As we near the end of Conservative rule, it is necessary to return for a moment to its beginning if we are to understand the full scale and nature of this betrayal. Twenty years ago, in the mid-1970s, the Conservative Party decided it wanted to become a different kind of party and to make this country into a different kind of place. Its new leaders, notably Margaret Thatcher and Keith Joseph, turned their back on the brand of one-nation Conservatism represented by such figures as Harold Macmillan (whose social sympathies and economic outlook had been shaped by the conditions in his Stockton-on-Tees constituency in the 1930s) and on the shared assumptions that underpinned the post-war mixed-economy welfare state. These New Conservatives, as I shall call them, promised to take the British people on a bracing ideological journey from which they would emerge with economic vigour and social health. Amid the turmoils and tribulations of the time, in 1979 the electorate voted (just) to take the ride. As the electorate is now being asked to travel even further and faster along the same road, it is a good moment to pause and inspect the wreckage so far.

Let me briefly remind you what was being said, claimed and promised by those New Conservatives who took over their party twenty years ago (and whose successors have

11

completed the capture today). Anyone with a strong stomach and a taste for irony can find a potted version in the 1979 Conservative manifesto, but here I offer the sophisticated version. The curse of the age was said to be 'socialism', which had evidently also infected the Conservative Party. It was the cause of unemployment, crime, inflation, family breakdown and every ill under the sun. Its concern with such misguided notions as social justice and equality eroded personal responsibility and destroyed enterprise. Its belief in collective action produced excessive taxes and a bloated state. The remedies flowed from the analysis. The state should be cut back, taxes should be reduced, inequalities allowed to flourish, and the market unleashed. Then came the promise: the consequence of pursuing such a course would be nothing less than an economic miracle, as enterprise and incentive worked their effects, while an ordered stability would descend upon society as individual responsibility replaced public provision.

So that was the prospectus and the promise. Now consider what has actually happened, for what has happened provides the setting in which lives are today being lived and this coming election fought. It is difficult to know whether the failures or the successes are more lamentable. I want to be as fair as I can be. The world before 1979 was not a halcyon age of cakes and ale, although to many it will now seem like a lost haven of security and stability. Some of the unwelcome changes that have damaged our society, such as the loss of traditional jobs and the erosion of settled communities, are part of wider trends that have made their presence felt elsewhere; but the nature of the response has mattered too. The present cyclical recovery of the economy, from the black hole of the last Conservative recession, is much to be welcomed; but it should not be confused with the requirements for long-term economic strength. And, a final fairness, some of what has been done since 1979 needed to be done and I hope would have been done by a Labour Government too.

But fairness has its limits. When all the allowances have been made and all the caveats entered, the fact remains that the Conservative promise has turned out to be a chimera. It has failed even in its own terms, but in those areas where it has succeeded the consequences have been still worse. The promise to launch an assault on 'over-government' has turned into a dramatic extension of central state power, including the wholesale nationalization of services such as education. A commitment to 'deregulation' meets the reality of a Government that has churned out an average of 500 pages more legislation annually than its Labour predecessor (and a further 500 pages more of secondary legislation each year). Far from bringing taxes down, the burden of taxation has steadily and sometimes sharply risen during the Conservative years (including the biggest tax hike in peacetime history *after* the last general election), its distribution has become more unfair and it has been extended to areas (as with the imposition of VAT on domestic fuel bills) previously free of tax. The independent Institute for Fiscal Studies provides the definitive verdict: 'The main fact about the tax burden since 1979 is that it has risen from 34.25 per cent to 35.75 per cent of national income.' The promised attack on welfare dependency has issued in a huge growth in the numbers of people now dependent on welfare benefits, and a social security budget that is swallowing up an ever greater share of public spending. From 23 per cent of government expenditure in 1979 (9 per cent of GDP), social security spending had increased to 31 per cent (nearly 13 per cent of GDP) by 1996, while one third of the population now lives in households which draw at least one of the major means-tested benefits – a figure that has doubled since 1979.

The attribution of crime to the pernicious effects of a culture of social democracy is mocked by a crime rate that has more than doubled since 1979 and is corroding the fabric of civilized life. The espousal of 'family values' confronts the record of a period in which family breakdown has sharply accelerated, more seriously in Britain than elsewhere, with unprecedented numbers of divorces and of children living without two parents. Those who recall the 'Labour isn't working' posters with which the Conservatives attacked the Labour Government's employment record in 1979 will be able to make their own comparisons with the much bleaker position today. They should also reflect on the fact that the Conservatives have altered the way in which unemployment figures are calculated no fewer than thirty-one times, refusing to use international standards, and that the last time unemployment fell to its current level there were 800,000 more people *with* a job than now. The permanent revolution waged against the education system, with a new piece of education legislation in almost every year that the Conservatives have been in power, ends in the dismal discovery that a generation of children are leaving primary school without a grounding in basic skills.

It is a depressing story. It is also a story about the consequences of economic failure. No doubt the Conservatives would have liked to slash taxes, reduce the share of spending on welfare payments and create more jobs; but the effect of their economic failure has been to make such objectives unattainable. It is the price of their failure. The promise was of an economic renaissance; the reality is of an economy that has lagged behind our main competitors in terms of growth and investment since 1979, achieved a trade deficit in manufactured goods for the first time since the Industrial Revolution, and caused us to drop from thirteenth to eighteenth in the international league of national incomes. We invest

14

less than any other OECD (Organization for Economic Cooperation and Development) country, while the growth of the economy of only about 1.9 per cent a year since 1979 compares badly with over 3 per cent in the period between 1969 and 1973. In the words of *The Economist* (21 September 1996): 'So much for the Thatcher miracle.' The growing concern about our competitive position is entirely justified, but the tragedy is that it has taken so long even to recognize the problem. Whole swathes of British industry were casually driven to the wall in the first Conservative recession of the early 1980s, the victims of a dogma that showed a reckless disregard for the needs of the real economy, while the economic mismanagement that produced the last Conservative recession in the early 1990s is the indispensable context within which the current pre-election recovery has to be set.

These failures are spectacular enough, but it is where the New Conservatives have succeeded that the consequences are even more direly damaging. They promised an end to the post-1945 concern with fair shares, equality and social justice. A vibrant economy would require lots more rich people and lots more poor people. 'It's our job to glory in inequality' was Mrs Thatcher's rallying cry to her ideological storm troopers. In more sophisticated language, a theory of 'trickle down' was advanced to explain the mysterious alchemy by which an economy liberated from tiresome concerns about equity and redistribution would generate a dynamism that would eventually bring benefits for all. *Enrichez-vous* would mean *enrichez tout*. Cedric Brown's British Gas bonanza would somehow find its way into my elderly constituent's handbag.

Well, the theory has been put to the test and the results are now in. In one sense the policy of the New Conservatives has been a resounding success. As report after report has now documented in devastating detail, Britain has been

15

turned into a much more unequal society. (It is strange, by the way, that clever apologists for the new dispensation should want to dispute these findings, since this is merely the promised outcome of the medicine they prescribed.) There are more rich people and there are more poor people, and the gap between those at the top and those at the bottom has widened sharply. For the first time since the Second World War, during the 1980s the poor's share of Britain's national income fell and poverty increased. Between 1979 and 1993 the income of the poorest tenth of the population declined by nearly 20 per cent, while that of the richest tenth increased by some 61 per cent. By 1992/3, 14.1 million people (a quarter of the population) were living below half the national average income after housing costs, compared with 5 million people (9 per cent of the population) in 1979. In my own constituency in Staffordshire, 23 per cent of households have an income of less than £7,500 a year. More than 4 million children, three times as many as when the Conservatives came to power, are now officially living in poverty. The Rowntree Foundation's 1995 report, *Inquiry into Income and Wealth*, concluded: 'Income inequality in the UK grew rapidly between 1977 and 1990, reaching a higher level than recorded since the War.' A recent report from the United Nations Development Programme showed that Britain is now the most unequal country in the Western world, with the gap between the richest and poorest fifths of the population the same as Nigeria's and substantially greater than that of such countries as Ethiopia, Jamaica and Sri Lanka.

What makes Britain distinctive, in Western Europe at least, is that the position in which it finds itself is the deliberate outcome of its Government's policies and ideology. Its self-proclaimed mission was to glory in inequality. The problem is that the success of this policy has not been accompanied by the beneficent effects that were supposed to flow from it

16

in diffused prosperity and well-being. The only certain effect of the promotion of inequality turns out to be just that – inequality. Yet of course this is not quite so, for a society that is marked by more inequality and increased poverty will produce its own malign effects on the general quality of life in its midst. We might describe this as the 'trickle up' effect. Its operation can be seen and felt on every street and in every community in the land, as social cohesion is fractured and the precious glue that holds societies together as shared enterprises in which people have a stake starts to come unstuck. It makes neither economic nor social sense. Yet it is what the new breed of Conservatives set out to achieve, and what they have so catastrophically delivered.

But even now the story of these long Conservative years is not complete, for there is also the tragedy of the unique opportunities for national renewal that were available in this period and so wantonly squandered. At the time of the 1979 general election the clever pundits, pointing to the huge revenues that were about to flow into the Treasury from the black gold in the North Sea, predicted that the winning party could well stay in office for a decade or more. And so it has proved, except that what could not have been predicted was that at the end of such a period the country would have nothing to show for this divine largesse. Nor was this the only pot of gold that became available of course, for there was also the proceeds from the regular auction of the nation's assets as public industries were disposed of to private buyers. The revenues from these combined sources are of quite staggering proportions: some £128 billion in the case of North Sea oil and £80 billion of privatized public assets. This is the fiscal equivalent of an individual winning the national lottery on a roll-over week.

Where has it all gone? The tragedy is that it has simply been consumed as revenue, when it should have been seen as the opportunity for sustained investment. It could have been used for major infrastructural renewal (in the water industry, for example, which consumers are now paying dearly for, or in developing a modern integrated transport system), and for a massive investment in education. But the New Conservatives had set their ideological face against any such planned interferences with the 'natural' operation of markets and the opportunity was dissipated. Not only that, but the period ends with a Conservative Government presiding over another black hole in the public finances and a problem of public debt that has even closed down its options for substantial pre-election tax cuts. It is an extraordinary and dismal end to a period which offered such economic opportunities. It is scarcely surprising that it provokes a pervasive sense of let-down and betrayal.

There is an alternative, and much of the rest of what follows is concerned with just that. Moreover, it is an alternative that is genuinely new, different from both the Old Labour prescriptions of the 1970s and the New Conservative dogmas of the 1980s and 1990s. It is a new approach for a new world. But it only becomes available if the failures of the recent past are understood, and the perpetrators of those failures are dispatched from office. That is why it is necessary to attend to the betrayal first. Elections are moments when governments are held to account for their stewardship of the nation's affairs and this Government of bad stewards has lost the right to stay in office. There are many traditional Conservatives, including a raft of those Members of Parliament who have decided to stand down at this election as well as those who have left to join Labour or the Liberal Democrats, who also feel angry and betrayed at the takeover of their party by the zealots of the new right. It is already clear that this takeover will be taken a stage further after this election, the unlovely contenders for leadership already jostling for position in a party that has become a very different place from the party of Churchill, Butler, Macmillan and Heath. Its present state of barely suppressed civil war will then move into its final stage of bloody resolution, in a parliamentary party that will have become even more right-wing. As New Labour has occupied the radical centre of British politics, the New Conservatives have departed to its wilder shores. When Mrs Thatcher was deposed so brutally by her own side in 1990, the Conservatives, while cleverly avoiding the perils of a general election, liked to think that they had persuaded people that there had been a change of government. Indeed when the election did come in 1992, they had good reason to think that the trick had worked. But it is now clear that the choice of John Major was a non-decision by a divided party, which is why he hangs in suspended animation, there only in immobilized futility until the warring factions do what has to be done. It is not a pretty or an inspiring sight.

For many millions of people voting in this election, Conservative Governments are all they have known. My eldest son, who has just left school to go to university, has lived his whole life under Conservative rule. For nearly two decades Britain has been run by one party. No doubt that explains the tawdry arrogance of a regime that has grown accustomed to identifying the public interest with its own. Our political system badly needs the cleansing wind of fresh ideas and new people. Yet Conservative ministers persist in responding to each new policy disaster in a manner which suggests that they are unaware that they have been responsible for the nation's affairs for a longer period than any Government this century. Some of my colleagues in the House of Commons have developed the no doubt reprehensible but entirely understandable habit of greeting ministerial announcements and apologias with cries of 'Eighteen years'. With their ideological project in ruins, its founding premise exploded,

19

Why Vote Labour?

the Conservatives enter this election hoping to persuade the country to share in their own collective amnesia. They are likely to be disappointed. People remember too much to forget, or forgive, quite so easily.

THREE

New Labour, Old Values

If this election is about a reckoning with betrayal, it would be dishonest if Labour's own part in this story was not frankly acknowledged. For what has happened to the Labour Party is as crucial to this election as the travails of the Conservatives. This is the fifth consecutive general election in which the New Conservatism of a Thatcherized party has offered itself to the electorate. But it is the first election in which New Labour is the alternative. That, crucially, is what makes this time different. Many people will be voting Labour in this election, and many of those for the first time, not just because they are fed up with the Conservatives, but because they like the look of the New Labour Party.

In this situation the dishonest temptation is simply to settle for a happy contrast between New Improved Labour and the Tired Old Tories. Perhaps there are even some in Labour's own ranks, especially those who may believe that politics is a branch of marketing, who would prefer to settle for this. If so, they would be wrong; for unless people understand what has happened to Labour in recent times, they will not really understand why the party is entitled to their trust and support now. Indeed, to say that people 'like the look' of New Labour is to understate the significance of what has happened. For what has happened is not a make-over but a genuine transformation. Nor is it the product of a quick visit to a political restoration company, but of a long and often painful process of rethinking and reconstruction. It has required much courage and many risks along the way. But it has been accomplished and the party has been renewed. That is obviously good news for Labour, but, more important, it is good news for everyone who wants and needs an alternative to the kind of politics that has been able to do so much damage to this country for so long.

Let me be more honest than prudent. If the Conservatives have been guilty of betrayal, then so too has Labour. The Labour betrayal consisted in its failure over an extended and crucial period to be the kind of party, and to offer the kind of programme, that a majority of electors wanted to vote for. If the country has had to endure nearly two decades of one-party rule from the new dogmatists of the right, it is in no small measure because the forces of the centre-left made it so easy. Even though the Conservatives never succeeded in winning more than a minority of the popular vote (only 41.9 per cent in 1992), and despite the consistent survey evidence showing that the values of the New Conservatives were not the values of the majority of the British people, it has nevertheless been possible for a Conservative Government to stay in office since 1979. Labour has to accept its own share of the responsibility for this. It may have preferred to seek refuge in Brecht's remark about the need to elect a new people, but its duty was to become a new kind of party. That is what it has now done.

In the leadership election necessitated by the sudden death of John Smith in 1994, Tony Blair circulated a position statement to Labour MPs. Its language and message were unlike anything the party had heard before. There were no weasel words and cosy equivocations, just a set of blunt truths and stark challenges. For me there was one sentence in particular that stood out: it said that through four general elections the British people had been trying to tell the Labour Party something and that the time had come to listen and respond. This was a brave and bold assumption of responsibility for what had happened, a most un-politician-like reversal of the normal way in which parties think of voters, and an uncompromising call to action. From that moment it was clear that not only was Tony Blair a politician of a new and different kind but that, if he was elected, the Labour Party would never be the same again. And so it has proved. The simple and obvious fact, devastating to the Conservatives but a source of hope to everybody else, is that the arrival of Tony Blair has had a transforming effect not just on the Labour Party but on British political life as a whole. This election provides dramatic evidence of this. And the best is yet to come.

What were the messages that the voters had been trying during the 1980s to send to Labour? It is necessary to register this troubled history if the extent of the party's transformation is to be fully grasped. There was an assortment of messages. That a party that had turned in on itself in an orgy of sectarian strife was not fit to run the country (a lesson about to be taught to the Conservatives again now). That a party agenda that seemed to revolve only around more state control and higher taxes was out of tune with the times. That it was not enough to be a caring party if the caring could not be paid for or priorities clearly established. That a party that seemed to be the prisoner of outside interest groups could not pursue the public interest. That a party that represented producer interests could not properly represent consumer interests, not least in the public sector. That a party that seemed more interested in defending yesterday's economy than in creating the conditions for tomorrow's was on the wrong track. That a party whose instincts on so many

23

fronts appeared defensive and conservative was unlikely to
be a source of radical ideas. That a party that seemed to be
on an ideological trip from somewhere in the past (another
contemporary lesson for the Conservatives here) was increasingly irrelevant to a changed world. When put together, all
this meant that Labour had created for itself a massive
problem of trust and identity with the voters. It could not
be remedied merely by a few policy adjustments or cosmetic
improvements (though both were tried); it required nothing
less than a fundamental remaking of the party.

That is what the Blairite revolution has been about. The
messages have been listened to and acted upon. It is now
clear to all what Labour stands for, what kind of party it is
and what direction it is offering to the country. Some in the
party have found this a painful process, but it is inconceivable
that it could not have been. What is remarkable is how much
has been accomplished, more than was thought possible by
many both inside and outside the party, and what effects
this has had on the party's standing. It is as though millions
of people had been waiting for Labour to become the sort
of party they wanted to vote for; which is of course precisely
what they had been doing. The tragedy is that they had to
wait for longer than they should have done.

In that phrase of Yeats, Labour is 'changed, changed
utterly'. New Labour is not a neat marketing ploy but an
accurate description of a party reborn. It is now a party which
has enfranchised its individual members, at the expense of
the trade union power-brokers. In rewriting Clause Four of
its constitution (of which more in a moment) it has provided
a new statement of what it stands for. In producing a draft
of its election manifesto months before the general election,
it has done what no party has done before. In its determination to promise only what it can deliver, and deliver what it
promises, it demonstrates its seriousness. The reward for

24

such manifest virtue is that the party has attracted a record number of new members to its ranks, making it the only mainstream party in Europe with an expanding membership, with a large influx of young members. Its standing with the voters tells its own story. The contrast with the Conservative Party, its organizational and membership base withering, could not be starker.

But it is important also to understand what Labour has changed and what it has retained. In renewing and modernizing itself, it has not repudiated its past but rediscovered it. Labour is a young party, still not yet a century old. It is the only one of the major political parties in Britain that did not begin life in Westminster, needing the arrival of a wider franchise to force them to develop a broader base (which may explain why so many politicians still talk, absurdly if revealingly, of going 'out into the country'). Labour only arrived at Westminster as the outgrowth of a popular movement for improvement and reform. Its realists wanted more economic and social security, its idealists sought the good society; but what united them all was a commitment to making Britain a more decent place in which to live for all its citizens. That was always the core of Labour's belief system and remains so today. It is why Labour has been called the people's party.

It was a party I was born into rather than joined. That is a confession rather than a boast, since converts to a cause perhaps have rather more claim to be listened to. But the party I was born into, in a small boot- and shoe-making town in Northamptonshire, has always exemplified for me – far better than any books of history or theory – what the Labour Party really stands for. It was part of an interlocking network of community life: the chapels, the Co-op, the clubs, the friendly societies, the trade unions, the party. This network was peopled by men and women, extraordinary in their ordinariness, who simply got on with the business of mutual support and collective improvement. They wanted the best for themselves and their families, but knew that it made sense to join with others to get it. For them the Labour Party represented not high theory but deep common sense. It was practical social-ism. Of course that particular post-war world has changed almost out of recognition. It would be no more than a sentimental exercise in nostalgia to recall it, except for the fact that it provides a reminder of where the Labour Party came from and what it has always stood for.

It is when Labour has forgotten this that it has got into trouble, as it did so catastrophically during the 1980s. The reason why it was so important for Labour's renewal process to involve a review of Clause Four (no doubt an arcane mystery to most people outside the party, but a matter of totemic significance for some of those within) was that it obliged the party to rediscover what it stood for and believed in. In having to do this for itself, it made it better able to communicate it to others. The real problem with the old Clause Four was not that it seemed to commit Labour to nationalize everything in sight, though it did; but that it represented a classic confusion of means and ends. Policies are for changing, as circumstances and problems change. Values are for keeping, as the enduring reference point by which policy compasses are set. In its confusion of values with policies, ends with means, the Clause Four of 1918 was massively unhelpful. If socialism was really only about public ownership, then the old Soviet Union would have been the most socialist society on earth. Labour had long understood the absurdity of such a proposition, but it had not thought it necessary to translate this understanding into a new public philosophy. Tony Blair was widely advised to let sleeping dogs lie in this respect, advice which he wisely and bravely rejected. He knew that sleeping dogs had a nasty habit of waking up and biting you when you least expected it. But he also knew that Labour could not honestly claim to have renewed itself as a party unless it could tell people what it believed in.

It has now done just that. In a few simple but compelling propositions it has described its framework of values and beliefs: that a society of fairness and equal chances is to be preferred to one of privilege and discrimination; that individuals flourish best in a community that provides the conditions for them to flourish; that self-improvement and collective improvement are not opposites but complements; that a dynamic economy and a decent society are mutually reinforcing. Such propositions are elementary in their obviousness, but it is a measure of their neglect and disavowal in recent times that they come back to us with a fresh force now. Perhaps it needed experience of the consequences of proceeding on a different basis for nearly two decades to remind us of what we once knew.

When Labour produced its new statement of what it stood for, a grudging editorial in the London *Evening Standard* offered perhaps the most significant tribute. It acknowledged that Labour had put into words what most people in this country believed. That is not a bad starting-point for a political party that wants to govern the country. The party's betrayal had not been its ditching of obsolete ideological baggage, but its failure for so long to become the kind of party that enough people wanted to vote for. In putting right that failure, it has rediscovered its essential self. New Labour is the authentic expression of the impulses and values from which the party was born. But Labour's modernization and renewal, the indispensable fact of this election, is only the necessary precondition for its ambition to modernize and renew the country. It is not quite true, though sometimes said, that running the country is easier than running the

Why Vote Labour?

Labour Party. What is true is that Labour is back in business as the people's party; and that it has thereby reclaimed the right to ask to be entrusted to run the country.

FOUR

What Matters Now

Every general election tends to be described as the most important of modern times. The truth is that, while all general elections matter, some clearly matter more than others. Some are 'shaping' elections, where a choice is made and a course set that endures not just for four or five years but for a generation. The 1945 general election was like that, establishing the framework for the post-war world. The 1964 election also qualifies, as a modernizing moment. And 1979 was emphatically such an election, breaking the long post-war settlement and charting a radically different course. There is no doubt that this election will be an addition to the list. In other words, it matters.

It is as well to be quite blunt about why this is. A fifth Conservative term would confirm Britain as a single-party regime, one freely chosen by its people but such a regime nevertheless. This would affect and infect all its institutions and its whole culture. The only opposition that counted would come from within the ranks of the ruling party. Assorted single-issue groups would still huff and puff, some journalists and broadcasters would continue to irritate ministers, Her Majesty's Opposition would go on performing its oppositional routine, but everyone would know that the nature of the game had changed. We already have a glimpse of such a world, but this is merely the palest of imitations of what it would actually be like. I do not conjure up this prospect simply in order that people will be moved to reject it. While it may be a good reason for not wanting the Conservatives to continue in office (and it is), it is not a good enough reason for voting Labour.

The implications for Labour of the sort of scenario just sketched would be dire. It would mean that, even after renewing itself from top to bottom, it had still been rejected by the voters. It would have nothing else left to do and nowhere else to go. Of course, I do not believe for a moment that this will happen, but there should be no dissembling about what is at stake. But there is much more at stake even than this. For the arrival of a single-party regime would mean not only that had Labour's great project of renewal failed, but that the majority of the British people had decided that they wanted to continue on the ideological course first embarked upon in 1979. More than this, a decision would have been made to sign up to an intensification of that project, as the New Conservatives of the radical right consolidated their grip on their party and got an unfettered hold on the country. This is a truly frightening prospect; but it is also why this is a defining election.

It is crucial that people should understand the nature of the choice that is now before them. It is not merely a choice of party, nor even of policy, but of values, ideas and directions. The choice that is made now will set the framework within which particular policy decisions are made on everything from health to education and from welfare to the constitution. There is a fundamental difference of approach and belief between the New Conservatives and New Labour and the British people are now being asked to choose between them. Of course the facts of the world in which policy decisions are made exert their own inexorable discipline, even if the heady rhetoric of politicians on the stump sometimes suggests otherwise, but the fact that political choices are always constrained does not mean that they are not real ones. The remark attributed to one Australian politician that, while there might only be an inch of difference between a Labour Government and a Government of the right, it was 'an inch worth living in', both makes the point well and perhaps endows it with an unnecessary cynicism. There are moments and places when an inch can feel like a mile and this is one of them.

There have been some general elections in the past when, although the contending parties have differed in emphasis and outlook, they have shared enough in common to make the election a contest between rival claims about respective abilities to achieve broadly consensual objectives. This is emphatically not the case in this election. An acid test to apply to any political party is to make a judgement about what it would really like to do if it could, without having to worry about electoral constraints and consequences. Honesty compels me to concede that there have been moments in the past when I would not have liked this test to have been applied to the Labour Party. But apply the test to the Conservatives now, then combine it with the actual removal of constraints that would come with fifth-term triumphalism, take a stiff drink to a dark room and imagine the future. Fortunately, this exercise has already been conducted and by no less than the Olympian intellects that reside within HM Treasury. When the product of their reflective analysis found its way into the columns of *The Times* a few months ago, Conservative ministers were understandably embarrassed. Kenneth Clarke tried to brush it aside as a spasm of teenage doodling, but this merely confirmed his beleaguered position as the ideological zealots prepared to sweep past him. For the picture that the Treasury paper painted, of a country in which public services and the welfare state had been privatized almost out of existence, is precisely the picture to be found in every handbook of the New Conservative radical right.

Consider, as an example, a recent work by the Conservative MP Alan Duncan (who is also an aide to the chairman and propagandist-in-chief of the Conservative Party, Brian Mawhinney). It is a manifesto for the minimal state of libertarian individualism. Not only are we to be 'liberated' into drugs, but 'freed' from a whole range of other collective responsibilities. ('In an atmosphere of upheaval it should be possible to close down entire departments of State and withdraw from whole areas of State activity, rather than rely on chipping away . . .') Public spending, which even after eighteen years of Conservative rule stands at over 40 per cent of GDP, is now to be slashed to a residual 15–20 per cent as services such as public education are 'liquidated' (*Saturn's Children*, 1995). In case it is thought that this kind of slash-and-burn approach to public spending is untypical, it should be remembered that one of John Major's many appeasements of his right wing has been to promise a public spending target ceiling of 35 per cent of GDP. The task of containing public spending within affordable limits, and above all the task of reducing unproductive expenditure, is an inescapable problem for any government; but that is not what is at issue here. Nor is it even a matter of the intellectual merits of the argument about the relationship between the size of public spending and the rate of economic growth. When the evidence on this was recently reviewed by *The Economist* ('Slimming the State', 2 December 1995), it concluded: 'In Britain . . . it is no longer right to assume simply that public spending is bad, private spending good. It may make political sense for the government to try to push public spending below 40 per cent of GDP, but doing so at the cost of services does not obviously make economic sense.' This confirms that what is at issue is not an economic argument but an ideological ambition.

And it is this, more than the line-by-line comparisons of party manifestos, that represents the defining choice in this election. It is about whether people want to accept or reject the 'private good/public bad' philosophy of the New Conservatives; whether we want to approach the social and economic problems facing us on the basis of a one-nation inclusiveness or in a *sauve qui peut* spirit of a fragmented individualism; and whether we want to affirm or deny a politics of shared purposes and common values. If one set of choices is made, as I argue in the next chapter, the basis exists for a new radical consensus; if another set, then we are locked into the trajectory mapped out in that piece of Treasury futurology. This is our choice, now. Let there be no doubt that tough policy decisions flow from each, but let there equally be no doubt that there will be different policies with different consequences depending upon the shaping choice that is made.

This may be the moment, alas, to turn to John Redwood, putative leader of the Conservative Party and scion of the radical right. 'Cutting taxes,' he proclaims, 'is a moral proposition' (*The Times*, 22 September 1995). What an extraordinary, and revealing, statement this is. If there is still anyone in need of evidence about the nature of the choice now on offer, this provides it. It also evidences a confusion of ends and means on a scale that far exceeds anything the left has ever been able to achieve. Cutting (or for that matter, raising) taxes may be sensible or desirable in particular circumstances, above all in relation to the state of the public finances (currently dire), but to elevate this kind of policy decision to the status of an *a priori* moral proposition is both absurd and dangerous. It can, at best, only be a means to an end.

Why Vote Labour?

The requirement to behave decently to other people is a moral proposition; tax rates are not. What *is* a moral proposition is the duty to pay taxes, for this expresses a larger duty of citizenship. The fact that the New Conservative right is so silent on this is telling. Not only is it a silence that is corrosive of the idea of common citizenship, it is intended to be. If we are looking for examples of contemporary moral decline, here is a prime candidate.

Having entered the minefield of tax and spend, with electoral shells being lobbed furiously into it from all sides, it is necessary to linger for a dangerous moment in order to understand the real issues at stake. It seems to me that people are way ahead of the politicians on all of this. They know that, while it would be delightful to be able to combine minimal taxes with high-quality public services, this box of delights is not a real-world combination. They know that desirable things (like a good education system and a comprehensive health service) have to be paid for and that a decent society therefore needs decent taxes. They also know that politicians who promise to bring taxes down are quite likely to put them up (the enduring lesson of the 1992 general election). They are wary both of enthusiastic tax-raisers and of reckless spending-cutters. These seem to me to be eminently sound instincts, far sounder than much of what the current electoral propaganda allows for.

The joker in this particular pack is always economic growth, or at least the prospect of it. Growth and its associated revenues opens up the possibility of reduced taxes *and* public spending increases, which is why the policies most likely to secure this elixir are necessarily at the centre of political debate. I shall argue later that Labour's stakeholder approach offers the best prospect here, a chance to break out of the low-growth stop-and-start trough that has characterized the Conservative years; but for the moment I am more concerned to avoid the delusions that so conveniently dissolve the hard choices in this area. While it is the case that a sustained increase in the domestic growth rate of a seemingly modest half of one per cent would do more than anything else to open up the distributional choices available to us, it is also the case that such an achievement would be beyond anything that the British economy – for so long stubbornly anchored in a growth rate of around 2 per cent – has managed in its modern history. So we are left with unavoidable choices, and choices that carry values with them.

With improved growth, there would be distributional choices to be made between public spending and private consumption. Both are desirable; but I would expect a Labour Government, certainly more than a Conservative one, to ensure that public spending gets its proper share of a growth dividend. But there are choices to be made now too. The right has lost all credibility in terms of fiscal responsibility, in demanding tax cuts in the face of a gaping hole in the public finances (the Public Sector Borrowing Requirement (PSBR) for this financial year is running at some £4 billion above the Treasury forecast made in the November 1995 Budget). Not for the first time, pre-election folly is likely to bring post-election tears. But, equally, those who may still see tax increases as an ideological virility symbol have to confront the fact that not only are people already paying more tax than before, but the shape of the tax system now means that any serious revenue can only be raised by hitting the broad mass of ordinary taxpayers. The real task here, as Labour acknowledges, is to reduce the tax burden on low-income earners with a lower starting rate and, by increasing allowances, to take a raft of them out of tax altogether (contrasted with the Conservative priority of abolishing inheritance and capital gains taxes for the wealthy). This is why an old politics of tax and spend has to come to terms with a new reality.

But if Labour is honest about that, I should like to be as honest about the defining choices that remain on this front. I mention three briefly, all bearing directly on this election and its outcome. First, there is the whole question of whether the citizens of Western societies are prepared to continue to make collective provision through the tax system (or compulsory equivalents) for a range of services. The New Conservative right hopes that they will not be so prepared. It will remain the task of the Labour Party to make sure they have a choice. In the simple and direct words used by the Real World Coalition of over thirty voluntary groups, 'taxation can make everyone better off'. Second, there is the issue of fairness. The tax system has become markedly more unfair at the hands of the Conservatives (only those earning more than £64,000 pay less tax now than in 1979, everyone else is paying more) and Labour will want to make it more fair. Third, a related but broader issue, we have to decide whether taxation is still to be seen in redistributive terms. This used to be an axiom that those with the broadest shoulders should carry the heaviest burden. The Conservatives have taken a different view, with the consequences already described, and this election will determine which view is to prevail. Labour has rightly rejected any return to the penal levels of taxation that were once the norm, just as it is clear that tax levels have to stay within international parameters, but this does not and should not mean a rejection of the principle of redistribution. For example, a modest increase in taxation for those at the top end would not yield a pot of gold, but it would be a visible reaffirmation of the redistributive principle – especially if, as with Labour's other proposals, its proceeds could be directly tied to a specific beneficiary. I can well understand why Labour should be extremely wary about all this, in view of the mischief made by the Conservative misinformation machine, but I have a hunch that the British people would like to see a modest dollop of redistribution after the reverse-flow extravagances of recent times. They have learned the hard way about the real politics of tax and spend.

These are merely examples of the way in which particular policy choices have larger values buried within them. Elections are moments to be explicit about these. There is a clear choice here between the ethical basis of the New Conservative and New Labour projects, with very different consequences for policy and practice. Of course, the intellectual and political battle between left and right, progressives and conservatives, has in one form or another shaped the political life of the West over the whole two centuries since the French Revolution. But it has now entered a new phase, especially in Britain and the United States, as the New Conservative right has shed itself of the restraining civic understandings of an older conservative tradition and remodelled itself as a theory and practice of market individualism. In thinking of society only in individualistic and market terms (for ever captured in Margaret Thatcher's notorious remark about there being 'no such thing as society'), it has repudiated the idea of society as a common enterprise. In elevating the private, it has devalued the public. In trumpeting private responsibility, it dismisses collective responsibility. In turning citizens into consumers, it corrodes the basis of civic life. The catastrophic consequences of proceeding in this way have been well expressed by the political theorist, John Gray: 'The subversive effects of unhampered market institutions on traditional forms of life makes free-market conservatism an inherently unstable and, over time, a self-undermining political project.' This verdict is all the more telling in that it comes from someone who once embraced the tendencies whose consequences he now indicts so ferociously.

Yet the consequences flow inexorably from the presuppositions. If it is believed that there is no such thing as society, and policies are constructed on this basis, then there soon will be no such thing as society. The glue will have come unstuck. Anguish about the consequences from those who did the unsticking (of the kind that is in evidence now) is disingenuous. Complaints about a broken window come ill from those who supplied the ball. But whereas a broken window is easily mended, a fractured community is not. There is something truly alarming about the way in which the New Conservatives in Britain have worshipped at the shrine of the New Conservatives in the United States; as well as the general way in which the United States – a society which still asserts its freedom to pay little more than a dollar a gallon to drive its planet-polluting cars while 10 million American children now have no health insurance at all – is regarded as a model for emulation. Even Jack Kemp, last year's Republican vice-presidential candidate, felt obliged to warn his party about the perils of a policy of 'small hearts and big prisons'.

The remark reminds me of something said to me last year by a man who runs a small but successful family building firm in my constituency. We were at a little ceremony to mark the opening of a new toilet block at a primary school. The school in question is a beacon of hope and community in the middle of a deprived and demoralized estate. It had been a long struggle to get its appallingly insanitary toilets replaced, and the builder's firm had done the work. As we chatted, he described to me how his view of the world and of politics had gradually changed. Much of his recent and highly lucrative work had been in building extensions to the county prison. He contrasted this with the effort involved in getting new toilets for a school in a community that had nothing. 'I suppose I'm doing all right,' he said, 'but I can see that we can't go on like this.' It's those words again. At some point the 'I' and the 'we' inevitably come together.

It is no exaggeration to say that this election is the moment when we decide whether we do go on like this. There is a defining choice to be made. It is not a technical choice, but a moral one. It goes to the heart of the philosophical difference between the parties. What Labour stands for is a politics of community, a belief that we are all in it together, that society is a matter of shared obligations and mutual responsibilities. It is perfectly possible not to believe this. There are other choices available; and we are currently living under such a choice. But we are also living with the consequences of that choice. If we believe that human beings are merely disconnected atoms and that societies are no more than markets, then we are relieved of the need to organize our affairs on the basis that we are members one of another. All notions of one-nation inclusiveness, equity and justice can safely be discarded and, not being all in it together, we are fully entitled to kick away any ladders we manage to climb. In the absence of any ladders, we can simply kick over the traces. The question is whether we want to live in a society like that.

This election will provide the answer. That is why it matters. Labour's alternative is what I call 'communalism'. This is not a nostalgic yearning for a world that is lost, nor a desire to compress the rich diversity of modern life into an imposed shape. But it is an affirmation of mutuality and solidarity as the basis of social life. It finds its simplest but most enduring expression not in grand theories or dense theologies but in the kind of sentiments found in Robert Burns ('a man's a man for a' that') or the Putney debate of the English civil war ('the poorest he that is in England has a life to live as the greatest') or the ethical socialism of

Why Vote Labour?

R. H. Tawney ('because men are men, social institutions . . . should be planned, as far as possible, to emphasize and strengthen, not the class differences which divide, but the common humanity which unites, them'). It requires an initial and indispensable act of moral choice, but from this foundation other propositions follow. That a society will be stronger and happier if it includes rather than excludes. That individuals thrive best in a supportive and cohesive community. That we can achieve collectively much that we could not secure individually. This election provides an opportunity to rediscover some old truths after years of systematic neglect. Unless we get this right, we shall get much else wrong.

FIVE

Consensus for Radicals

Without a broad agreement on ends, what we believe in as a society and what we want to achieve, then it is unlikely that we shall develop the effective means to tackle the problems and challenges we face. If confirmation was needed of this elementary truth, the experience of the past two decades has supplied it in dismal abundance. But the point can be made much more positively, in a way that is directly relevant to the situation in which we find ourselves now. With a new consensus on aims and objectives, it would be possible to bring a whole new spirit of innovation and radicalism to the task of policy and implementation. This is the prize and the opportunity that the renewal of Labour has now opened up. For the first time in the political experience of most people voting in this election, the opportunity exists to break free from the sterile categories within which political debate in Britain has been imprisoned for so long.

There are already signs that a new consensus of ideas and applications is in the making and that Labour is its carrier. While the right is in intellectual retreat, there is a renaissance of thinking among progressives on the centre-left. As David Willetts has gloomily acknowledged, the last year has been 'a bad year for Conservatives fighting the battle of ideas' (*Blair's Gurus*, Centre for Policy Studies, 1996). But what is emerging is not a soggy consensus of lowest common denominators, which would be ruinous; rather, a radical consensus in which new responses to a new world are being developed. It is also a consensus in the making, still unfinished, without a tidy label. Tributaries flow in from different policy areas – such as economics, welfare, education, crime and political reform – and contribute to the evolving shape of the whole. A new language of stakeholding, community, inclusiveness and responsibility increasingly defines the terrain. Old categories are subverted and new connections are established. The most important connection of all is between these developing ideas and the manner in which people are beginning to think about their society in ways that demand a quite new response. As Melanie Phillips has put it: 'People are feeling their way towards a civic organization that is neither driven by individualism nor state control in order to synthesize freedom and responsibility' (the *Observer*, 8 September 1996). This is where the developing political agenda is to be found. And it is New Labour's territory.

Having so far here avoided anything that looks like manifesto writing, I now allow myself one lapse. This is partly to prove that the agenda I have just described is not merely my own, but also because the paragraph I am about to quote seems to me to be a rather good summary of what this new agenda consists of. It comes from Labour's draft manifesto (*New Labour, New Life for Britain*) that was published last year. It describes a politics that is 'neither old left nor new right', an approach that 'leads from the centre, but is profoundly radical', and then spells out what this means:

'We should not be forced to choose between state control of the economy and letting the market do it all; between higher levels of tax and spend and dismantling the welfare state; between a society that denies enterprise and one in which we step over bodies sleeping in doorways; between monolithic, centrally delivered public services and those so bad that anyone who can afford to opts out of them; between head-on conflict between bosses and workers and denying employees any rights at all; between excusing criminal behaviour and ignoring the conditions that give rise to it; between indifference to family breakdown and trying to recreate the family life of 50 years ago. The political agenda of Britain simply does not need to be like this.'

Indeed it does not; but the tragedy is that it has been like this for so long. The alternative is not to want to have your cake and eat it, but to understand that it is possible to have more than one good thing at the same time. A politics of synthesis and balance is not an easy evasion of difficult choices; it is a tough repudiation of the tyranny of a sterile politics of false opposites. State or market; individual or community; freedom or responsibility: these are just the pivotal antinomies that cry out for an 'and' instead of an 'or'. There is something distinctive, and distinctively disabling, about a political tradition in Britain in which the contesting arguments have simply talked past each other. Where there could have been constructive engagement, there has been a sustained dialogue of the deaf. In part this is a malign product of the particular way in which we organize our politics (on which more later); but it is also the burden that is carried by a particular history. What Orwell called the 'accursed itch of class' in Britain has been a perennially troublesome irritant in so many areas, from education to industry, thwarting common purposes and preventing concerted strategies. Yesterday's battles, and the cultures in which they were embedded, still dominate responses to too many of today's challenges. In both ideas and policies, we have been prisoners of the past.

Why Vote Labour?

We have paid a considerable price for this. While post-war Germany was constructing a successful 'social market' economy, with an excellent system of technical education as one of its underpinnings, we were still slugging it out on the industrial battlefield and feeling a surly resentment at the way in which history had clearly cheated us. While Europe started building common institutions to ensure that the continent's future would be better than its past, we preferred to lull ourselves with the fading echoes of empire. In area after area, issue upon issue, we have seemed unable to break out from an inheritance of entrenched positions and limited political imaginations. For too long politics in Britain has been on intellectual auto-pilot. The opportunity now exists to make a decisive break with this.

For example, when Tony Blair first talked about being 'tough on crime and tough on the causes of crime', at one level it was just a nice politician's phrase (or should that be 'politician's nice phrase'?). But what was remarkable, and revealing, was the way in which it soon became more than that. For what it represented was precisely a breakout from the inherited categories within which the political debate about crime had been locked for so long and with such sterility. It did not have to be like that, but it was. In being like that, it closed off the opportunity for new approaches. There were those who insisted that crime was only an expression of social deprivation and there were those who insisted that it was only an issue about law and order; but while this familiar routine of mutual antagonism continued, the chance of making any serious progress was unnecessarily limited. Yet what was needed was concerted and integrated action on both fronts (and on others). Only the present Government, or that part of it represented by Michael Howard, persists in denying the evidence of the police, of research and of common sense on the link between poverty, unemployment and crime; but with a new prison now needed every three weeks, the failure of this blind-eyed approach is evident to all. On the other hand, merely to repeat a mantra about the social causation of crime is to fail to explore the new approaches to prevention, punishment and community-enforcing that are so obviously needed.

Yet the issue of crime is only an example of the general point. The fact that a politician's utterance in which a familiar 'or' was replaced by an unfamiliar 'and' could be received not as a bland truism but as a revelatory breakthrough is a gloomy confirmation of the impoverished way in which we have been accustomed to thinking about a whole range of issues. Too often politicians have not thought openly about them at all. The more cheerful way of telling the same story is to recognize the potential that is unlocked once the old confining categories are disengaged from. Nor is this merely now a desirable option. The challenges of a transformed world make it a compelling necessity. The old ideological paradigms have collapsed and traditional compass settings no longer provide reliable guides to action. The fundamental value choice is immutable, but beyond that we all have to start thinking again, freshly and together. A new politics for a new world is not a smooth slogan but an inescapable obligation.

Nowhere is this more necessary than in the central argument about the respective roles of markets and states. This argument goes to the heart of political conflict in the modern world, but it is also the arena in which the basis for an emerging consensus can be glimpsed. In the British context, this would be a development of historic importance. A market economy is the most expedient way of organizing economic life and, with the collapse of the discredited and inefficient East European command economies, the world has no example of even a malfunctioning alternative. The idea that states are better than markets at doing most of what economies are required to do may still be believed by Arthur Scargill and a few others, but the rest of the world has moved on. Furthermore, in a world of ferocious global competition, those market economies which are most dynamic will be most successful. In being successful, they will be better able to deliver wealth, jobs and welfare to their people. When Labour commits itself to the creation of a dynamic market economy, as it does in its new constitution, it merely recognizes these obvious truths.

But if this recognition forms an essential part of a modern economic consensus, it does not comprise the whole. For what we still have to decide is what kind of market economy we want and what are the conditions for its success. This latter issue is returned to in the next chapter; here the focus is on the general framework of ideas and assumptions within which particular policies are cast. Unless there is a broad agreement on this framework, the basis will not exist for a sustained policy consensus. This requires that the left should learn something from the right, and the right something from the left, if the old arguments about markets and states are to be converted into a more positive form. The right has always proclaimed the virtues of markets, while the left had traditionally embraced the role of the state. A whole repertoire of arguments, the stuff of a hundred years of politics, sustains each position. They are good and important arguments too. The problem with them, especially in Britain, is that they have been conducted on such doggedly separate tracks that they have rarely come together in a way that has made mutual learning possible. What the right can teach the left is something about the merits of markets and the infirmities of states; what the left can teach the right is something about the merits of states and the infirmities of markets. A radical consensus requires that both kinds of lesson are learned. Then it becomes market *and* state, private *and* public; and with such coupling comes innovative policy possibilities.

In the past these arguments have largely turned on the question of ownership. This coined the term 'mixed economy' as a description of a doctrine of separate ownership spheres. Ownership still matters, especially when privatization is driven into areas (such as water, railways and the Post Office) where it sensibly does not belong, but the context has clearly changed. A modern mixed economy has to fuse market and state, private and public, in much more dynamic ways. An obvious example is the opportunity that exists for Labour to inject new ideas into the stalled private finance initiative, or to promote forms of ownership that straddle the old categories of 'public' or 'private', or to develop a more satisfactory regulatory system for the privatized utilities, or to sponsor innovative urban regeneration and housing partnerships. But we have to clear some intellectual ground first. This means recognizing that it is not sensible for the right to be deaf to arguments about the deficiencies of markets, nor sensible for the left to be uninterested in arguments about the shortcomings of states. We need to combine the left's critique of the market with the right's critique of the state if we are to move into more fertile policy territory than we have occupied in the past. The market is a wonderful servant but a lousy master. The state expresses a public interest but it carries its own private interests too. Swap false opposites for combined truths and new directions are opened up.

Let us bring such abstract discussion down to earth. For the fact is that a radical consensus of this kind only becomes available to us if those blocking it are removed. The block from the left has been removed in the passage from Old Labour to New Labour; but the block from the New

Why Vote Labour?

Conservative right is firmly in place and prevents progress being made. The neo-liberal fixation with the market produces an ideological blindness to the need to ensure that market outcomes serve the public interest, to the role that an intelligent state can play in enabling a market economy to perform more successfully, and to an understanding that there are spheres of activity where market principles are entirely inappropriate. Hardly a day passes without the Office of Fair Trading or a City regulator identifying a failure of markets to protect consumers or investors, yet the zealots of the new right are content simply to chant their deregulatory mantra. The real issue is not whether there is too much regulation or too little, but whether particular regulation is sensible and necessary. Equally, what people need to know is that both private (market) power and public (state) power will work in their interest, in a context where – as with the privately owned, publicly regulated utilities, or the publicly funded, privately controlled pension and insurance funds that own most of the economy – old distinctions prove ever more elusive. The development of 'charter standards' in public services is wholly to be welcomed (and the process needs to be taken much further), but there is no reason at all why similar service standards should not be applied to private sector services too (for example, to ensure that trade protection schemes protect consumers far more effectively than they currently do). In the dynamic world of broadcasting and telecommunications, there is an evident and urgent public interest need to ensure that those who control the technologies do not also control access, erode standards and reduce genuine diversity.

The whole area of the public services cries out for a different approach. Here there really is the basis for a radical consensus within our grasp if we have the energy and imagination to reach out for it. The left has had to learn that public services are not run for the benefit of those who work in them but for the benefit of those who use them and depend upon them. It is extraordinary that anyone claiming to be on the left should ever not have understood this, for those who most believe in public services should also be those who are most assiduous in ensuring that such services are as effective in their operation as they can possibly be. Too often the demand for 'more resources' (always needed, sometimes desperately so) has functioned as a substitute for a more difficult agenda. The proper defence of professionalism (and it needs defending) has sometimes looked more like a defence against proper accountability. One of the great achievements of Labour's new thinking has been to enable it to reclaim the public service principle, badly in need of restoration and restatement, while not confusing this with old models of public service organization and delivery.

What this means is that it can build upon at least some of the 'new public management' changes of recent years. The imperative to run services as efficiently as possible will (and should) press as hard on a Labour Government as on any other. The opportunities afforded by the purchaser/provider split to clarify responsibilities and improve delivery systems should continue to be developed (as in education, where it would be possible to have local education commissions – perhaps directly elected – commissioning education services of specified standards from schools). But Labour's approach to public services, the basis for an innovative radicalism, will not be contaminated by the features that have characterized the approach of the New Conservatives. Three features in particular have been the source of the contamination: first, the dominating belief that the main task of government in relation to the public sector was to make it cost less; second, an obsession with structures at the expense of purposes; and, third, an ideological attachment to market mechanisms as the only route to public service reform. In combination, these features have prevented – and will continue to prevent – a sustained programme of public service improvement on an agreed basis. Yet that is what we need.

If there is any doubt about the character and consequences of the Conservative approach, the evidence exists on all sides. The cost-cutting preoccupation has produced the confusion of efficiency and effectiveness rooted in a theology of blind-eye accounting. One small example makes the larger point. My parents are in their late eighties and, though managing on their own, are increasingly frail and need more support. When their refuse collection was contracted out, they were told that the bin would no longer be collected from their house but would have to be taken out to the road. Struggling to do this one day last winter, on an icy garden path, my father fell and sustained head injuries that put him in hospital, followed by a period of home nursing. On some balance sheet it will doubtless show that the refuse collection service has become more efficient, but on any sane system of social accounting it would be shown to have transferred its savings into someone else's costs (and with interest). Such examples are endemic. This does not mean that it is wrong to contract out services; what it does mean is that dogma should not drive out sense.

The other features of the Conservative approach tell a similar story. In education especially, the structural obsession with breaking the back of the local education authorities and erecting the edifice of a national curriculum has been at the expense of a sustained focus on what really matters, namely, the quality of teaching and learning. As for the belief that the only solutions are market ones, to be imposed on services to which they are manifestly inappropriate, the case of the National Health Service is there for all to see. The effect has been to fragment the service in a way that progressively erodes the principles of equity and access upon which it was established (while generating an army of contract-chasing accountants in the process). Total expenditure on administration rose from 11.5 per cent of NHS spending in 1982/3 to 17.8 per cent in 1992/3, while there are now 20,000 more senior managers and 50,000 fewer nurses than there were in 1989. A dispassionate judgement on where this leaves the NHS has been provided by the BBC Social Affairs editor: 'We may be some way from the privatization of the provision of health care but there is now nothing in principle preventing large tracts of what has traditionally been provided by the NHS moving to the private sector. The mechanisms are in place – the main obstacle is political' (Niall Dickson, *Guardian*, 11 September 1996). What that means, in short, is that the future of the NHS will be decided in this election. If that sounds like electoral hyperbole, just ask yourself if the current breed of market Conservatives would ever have invented the NHS if it did not already exist. It represents a standing defiance of all they believe in, a public service more efficient than a private alternative and rooted in principles of equity and need. If direct political assault from without is difficult, they will undermine it from within.

It is precisely because Labour is uncontaminated by this ideological agenda that it can be genuinely radical in its approach to public services. Its overarching and ruthless commitment will be to quality and standards, and it will be interested in a whole variety of new mechanisms to empower and involve service users. Some mechanisms which are tainted in the hands of those who come to bury public services may even look very different when hands are clean. As with the new kind of mixed economy, an agenda for a radical consensus begins to open up. It is not an agenda for a return to the world before 1979, but it does restore the idea of

Why Vote Labour?

public service and reclaims the belief in purposive public action. Without these as its foundation, the hope for any kind of new consensus will prove illusory.

SIX

A Stakeholder Economy

I shall never forget the day that Littleton pit closed. As the last shift emerged into the crisp winter morning, a lone bagpiper began to play. Wives and children ran forward. People cheered and wept at the same time. The piper led a procession into town, the pit banners were held proudly aloft, and a community stopped in silent tribute and collective grief. It was the last pit on the Cannock Chase coalfield. Not on the Government's original hit list for closure, it had nevertheless been shut down with a cold brutality that a community will never forget or forgive. The men who had worked and fought for it, and all the people who depended on it, did not have to use the language of stakeholding to know that it was *their* pit.

Then I think of another and very different day, just a few months ago, when I was invited to open an extension to a small factory on a new industrial estate just a couple of miles from where this pit used to be. I had opened the original unit and been so impressed with the young company and its enterprising owner that I had kept in regular touch. It had developed an innovative system for making enclosed steel structures (including the vending kiosks on many London street corners) and was clearly a company with a future. By the time I opened the extension, it was employing forty people and hoping soon to double that number, and was exporting 95 per cent of everything it produced. I tell the story here not because its owner clearly liked what Labour was saying about a new culture of partnership for business (though he did), but because companies like this are the future for areas such as mine. They have innovative products, long-term support from the bank, close relations with their suppliers and customers, local authorities and private developers working to provide sites, a commitment to continuous training and an involved and valued workforce. It is exciting just to be near a company like this. They also know what stakeholding is and why it makes sense.

But the problem with companies like this is that there are far too few of them. In terms of jobs, it needs a dozen such companies just to match the loss of the pit. The Government's own White Paper on competitiveness identified the problem that in Britain there is a 'long tail' of poorly performing companies, but what is lacking is the energy and commitment to develop the kind of sustained partnership between government and business to drive up performance and competitiveness across the board. Apart from the ritual incantation about its 'supply-side measures', the Government devotes most of its energies in this field to declaring what it is *not* willing or able to do. Even to get a government that is conspicuously determined to play its full part in the country's economic and industrial renewal, and which sees the commitment to full employment not as an obsolete memory but as an urgent challenge, will seem and feel like a huge advance. Unless we are content just to build more prisons, and pull up more drawbridges, we had better make a collective effort to do all that can be done to ensure work and wealth for our people.

The fact that old-style interventionism is now rightly rejected does not mean that an intelligent state lacks a constructive role in a market economy. Only the ideologues of the New Conservative right are blind to market failures, but it is a blindness that costs us dear. Economies are to be judged by their success in meeting the needs of those who depend upon them; markets are a means to this end and not the end itself; some economies and some markets work better than others; there is a public interest in making sure that markets work well and that market failures are corrected: it would not be necessary to recite such truisms if we had not lived through a period in which they had been so deliberately obscured. Many of the factors that contributed positively to the success of that company in my constituency – the infrastructure provision, the training that was available, the role of long-term finance – are areas where public policy has an active and important part to play. It is extraordinary that an ideological disposition to believe that markets should not be interfered with should have the perverse conclusion that markets, firms and the economy as a whole should not be enabled to work better.

It is not the job of governments to play at being capitalists; but it is the job of government to do all it can to make sure that a capitalist economy works well and serves the public interest. Some old-fashioned socialists will maintain that this is impossible; some old-fashioned capitalists (even if disguised as New Conservatives) will maintain that this is undesirable; but the rest of us can and should get on with doing it. The success we make of it will determine the kind of economy, and the kind of society, we live in. Government needs a dynamic economy, but business also needs a decent society. The common enterprise of citizenship encompasses both.

A core function of government is to be a competent manager of the macro-economy. With two major recessions and a devaluation under its belt (a recent report from the National

Institute of Economic Research has identified the continuing scale of the damage from the *first* Conservative recession of the early 1980s) and a trail of economic incompetence in its wake, the Government is desperately hoping that the current upturn in the economy will last just long enough to see it through the election. There could scarcely be a more miserable verdict on the nature of the Conservative economic record than this. When Labour says it is determined to provide a stable framework of macroeconomic management over the long term, with clear and prudent rules for spending and borrowing, it is because it wants to escape from the experience of the past. But it is also because it does not want to cheat the future. The reckless erosion of the nation's capital assets by the Conservatives and high levels of borrowing have done just that (with net wealth declining from nearly £20 billion in 1979 to *minus* £152 billion at the end of last year). Although the precise relationship between inflation and growth rates is disputed, Labour's commitment to low inflation as a basis for sustainable growth is also a commitment to the long term over the short term.

But sound and stable macroeconomic management is only one indispensable part of a new economic strategy. This also needs to get to grips with the underlying factors in economic performance as a basis for improving the long-term prospects of the British economy. Again there is a developing consensus on much of this, always excluding those New Conservatives who seem to be in government only to tell us how little government can do. We have some of the best companies in the world, but we also have a competitiveness problem that comes from having too many mediocre ones. We have a history of world-leading invention, but have too often failed to translate this into commercial advantage. We have been a remarkably unified society, but have allowed a negative 'two sides of industry' approach to dog our industrial relations. We made the first industrial revolution, but an endemic short-termism has prevented us leading the next ones. The challenge now is to put in place a concerted strategy that has a real chance of making the future better than the past. The choice in this election, between the kind of stakeholder approach offered by Labour and the inertia-as-ideology approach represented by the Conservatives, could not be clearer.

Stakeholding offers the basis for a new kind of partnership in business. Charles Handy puts it like this: 'We should think of a business not as a piece of property owned by someone but as a living community in which all the members have rights and whose purpose is continued existence. Companies are communities of people united by common aspirations rather than a bundle of assets owned by shareholders.' But of course it is not just rights; stakeholding involves an acceptance of a mutuality of obligations too. In case this sounds like merely pious exhortation, or just to describe what good companies are already doing, it is as well to be clear about the ways in which traditional British practice makes a stakeholding approach harder than it should be. This may explain why, in a recent survey of senior managers undertaken by the Industrial Society, in 80 per cent of companies there was a considerable gap between what managers believed about the importance of stakeholding and ethical business and what their organizations actually did. Yet there is a growing body of evidence to suggest that ethical business is good business and that a commitment to long-term stakeholding makes more commercial sense than a commitment only to short-term share prices.

The British tradition, with its narrow focus on shareholding instead of stakeholding, stands apart from traditions to be found in much of continental Europe and Japan. The Conservatives rejoice in this and embrace the merits of what they describe as the 'Anglo-American' model of freebooting and deregulated capitalism, red in tooth and claw and ferociously repudiating wider responsibilities. That is their vision of the future. Yet, in the British case, it is a model that has given preference to finance over industry and short-term returns over long-term investment. Consider some of its distinctive features. In Britain companies pay dividends that are twice as high as in Germany and three times as high as in Japan. During the 1980s the share of profits going in dividend payments doubled; and even during the recession trough between 1990 and 1992, with profitability stagnant, dividends increased by 21.5 per cent. The focus on high returns to shareholders, and a takeover culture that intensifies pressure in the same direction, means that there is chronic short-termism and under-investment. A major casualty is long-term research and development; rates of return expected on investment projects are typically 30 per cent higher than in Germany; and acquisition rather than investment is the preferred route to company growth. While most shares are now held by institutional investors, these typically have very dispersed holdings and therefore, unlike in France and Germany, few major stakes in individual companies. The effect of this is that shareholding becomes essentially passive, as evidenced by the fact that less than 15 per cent of the votes of pension funds – the largest category of institutional investor – are actually cast at company annual general meetings.

The growing awareness that all is not well in the world of corporate governance has been reflected both by the Cadbury Committee, set up in the wake of such scandals as Polly Peck and Maxwell, and by the Greenbury Committee's wrestling with the public outrage provoked by the excesses of executive pay. The remuneration issue exposes the hole where accountability should be. Yet the Government refuses to show serious interest in such matters, just as it refuses to allow even the most spectacular financial scandals to erode its blithe attachment to the chaos that is self-regulation in the City. Its further refusal to countenance the sorts of measures proposed by Labour to ensure that the privatized utilities behave like public interest companies is part of the same story. Yet public interest, here as elsewhere, is the key: if corporate and market structures and cultures are not serving the public interest as they should, then public policy has a responsibility to try to improve matters.

Not only does stakeholding challenge an excessively narrow view of shareholder responsibility (already challenged, of course, by the public interest framework provided by consumer, employee, environmental, health and safety and company law), but it also points to the long-term benefits to companies themselves in combining their indispensable responsibility to shareholders with responsibility to the wider community of stakeholders that includes the customers they serve, the workers they employ and the localities they inhabit. One study by two Harvard professors (Kotter and Heksett) found that stakeholder companies grew four times faster and created eight times as many jobs as shareholder-first companies over an eleven-year period; while also showing an eightfold improvement in share price and a spectacularly greater growth in net income. As Robert Waterman puts it in his book, *The Frontiers of Excellence*, the conclusion is that 'companies which, perversely, don't put shareholders first do better for their shareholders than companies that only put shareholders first'. The best companies know this, but they inhabit an environment which makes the practice of it much more difficult than it needs to be.

While there is room for argument about the extent to which progress in this area is primarily a matter for cultural change or new laws, or whether it requires a mixture of both, what there is not room for argument about is that there is a public policy issue here. Only the New Conservative right (which these days means the Conservative Party itself) feels the need to deny that there is a problem or that government has a role to play. Cultural change often needs a spur and a kick, while the continued failure even to implement the Greenbury recommendations on executive remuneration packages suggests that something more than a gentle nudge may be required to alter corporate practices. The same applies to the long history of underinvestment, consistently lower in Britain than in other industrialized countries, that has produced the loss of domestic industries and technologies while foreign investors have moved in to fill at least some of the vacated space. It is good that they have, just as it is good that Japanese work practices have had a transforming effect on whole tracts of industry here, but what is not good is that it has required foreign companies to invest where domestic investors have feared or failed to tread. That is why it is sensible, through tax incentives and other means, to strengthen an investment and savings culture in Britain.

It has become a truism to say that, in the modern global economy, it is investment in human capital – in skills and training – that is the route to competitive success. But this is one truism that is true. We should always resist crude utilitarianism in thinking about education, the purpose of which is to open up all that civilization can offer to critical minds and informed spirits, but this need not also prevent us from recognizing it as the route to economic prosperity for individuals and to economic success for nations. It is the skills that we have, as individuals and as a country, that are now the key determinant of the kind of living we shall earn. The level of educational investment that has been taking place in the dynamo economies of east Asia is positively awesome. By contrast, the British record has been positively awful. It is a record of underachievement and underprovision, except for a minority; but whereas this was once just a national disgrace it has now become a national disaster. The fact that education spending as a proportion of GDP has actually declined since 1979, as social security spending has dramatically increased, tells its own dismal story. We need the platform of a high-achieving education system for all, upon which can be added a high-quality system of skills training and lifelong learning: we have had neither. Studies of comparative educational performance in key areas such as mathematics consistently show Britain trailing (only one in four sixteen-year-olds passes GCSEs in mathematics here, compared with two in three passing the equivalent in Germany and France), while a world competitiveness report in 1994 ranked Britain eighteenth out of the twenty-three OECD countries in terms of the availability of skilled labour (nearly two thirds of the British workforce have no vocational qualifications, compared with one in three in The Netherlands and France, and one in four in Germany and Switzerland). Here is perhaps the greatest Conservative failure of all, for it is where the future is being made. It is also where Labour's priority is clearest, both in its central commitment to drive up educational standards in schools and in its range of proposals (including innovative plans for individual learning accounts and for a University for Industry) to transform the world of training and skills. A new training culture in British business is an integral part of a new investment culture.

It can sometimes be misleading to talk about 'the economy', as though it was simply a single entity with participants of a similar character. Yet this is clearly not the case, even after making the usual distinction between the manufacturing and service economies. Not only do companies come in all shapes and sizes, but there is the internationally traded economy where global competitiveness is all, regional economies with their own networks and relationships, local service economies which are highly differentiated and largely self-contained, and the economy of the public sector which is different again. An intelligent government needs to make sure that it has appropriate policies for each. Two examples, where Labour has taken some trouble to develop relevant policies, make the point. There is, first, the growing evidence that thriving regional economies, with close support networks, are an important site of economic dynamism in countries; and that the failure to develop these kinds of regional networks and supports for business in Britain, an expression of the more general British curse of centralism, has been a major disability. The strong regional emphasis in Labour's approach to business is designed to tackle this, not least in the crucial matter of ensuring that a strengthened science base connects with technology-transfer routes much more effectively than in the past. Then, second, there is the pivotal small business sector, which in terms of job creation alone should make it central to any strategy for business (for example, small businesses that came through the recession between 1989 and 1993 increased their employment by 50 per cent, whereas large ones saw a drop of 6 per cent). But small businesses are also the places where entrepreneurship and innovation flourish and rugged self-employment is sustained. There is good reason to think that the future will be small. The job of government is to provide support and remove obstacles. The close relationship that Labour has already established with the small business sector – on issues such as the late payment of debt, anti-competitive practices, sources of finance and over-regulation – provides a good basis for constructive partnership in government.

This returns us to where we began: only companies can be the motor of economic dynamism and competitive success on which we all depend, but governments can oil the motor

and clear the tracks. Some governments do this more successfully than others. The indictment of the Conservative
Government in Britain since 1979 is not just that it has been
manifestly unsuccessful in this task, but that its ideological
outlook has prevented it from engaging seriously with it.
It has fulfilled neither of the two key responsibilities of
government as far as the economy is concerned: to provide
a durable framework of macroeconomic stability, the basis
for sustained demand and investment, and to ensure that all
the underlying ingredients for long-term economic strength
are in place. It has combined incompetence on one front
with the ideology of inertia on the other. Its belief that
markets necessarily solve their own problems, and that the
success of government is to be measured by the extent to
which it deregulates markets, prevents it from doing effectively the range of things that governments can and should
properly do.

This kind of approach is also quite unable to grapple with
the radical economic challenges that are now staring us in
the face. I am thinking in particular of the challenges that
come from unemployment and the environment (and of the
connections between the two). The truth is that we simply
do not know whether economies, left to their own devices,
can ever again provide stable employment for all those who
need it. Neither the mantra of deregulation nor the rival
mantra of training answers the question. What we do know
is that our society is paying a terrible price for continuing
high levels of unemployment, especially among the young
(and a third of all those without a job in Britain are under
twenty-five). The price is economic, social and human. A
job gives a stake in society; without it, both individuals and
societies are damaged. The evidence for this is all around
us. Labour's proposal to use the proceeds from a windfall
tax on the privatized utilities to fund a bold scheme for

putting unemployed young people into work or training is clearly right, as is the proposal to give tax rebates to employers who take on the long-term unemployed. As we look into the future, we may have to be more radical still. We have removed jobs from area after area (where are the bus conductors? Park keepers? Hedge cutters?) not because of the imperatives of global competitiveness but because of doubtful beliefs about efficiency. The public spaces in our society are increasingly denuded of people, at a social cost; many of the most pressing social tasks we require to be done (whether in caring for the growing number of elderly people, or working with young offenders) are people-intensive; yet we pay £10,000 a year in benefits and lost taxes to keep someone unemployed. At some point, which may not be far away, we might conclude that it makes more sense to provide or subsidize jobs, especially in the public and local service sectors of the economy, than to train for jobs that do not exist or to subsidize unemployment. The environmental imperative, forcing a rethink of the tax system to promote sustainable people-based technologies, also pushes in the same direction. In all of this government and markets are called upon to work together in innovative ways in the public interest.

Even to think in this way requires a government that is not so imprisoned within the limitations of its own ideology that it fails to see the real opportunities and challenges that now confront us. The Conservative Party's current appeal to the electorate is based on an invitation to look only at one politically engineered moment in the economic cycle and to forget about its ineptitudes of yesterday or its failures to build for tomorrow. The only vision it can offer is of Britain as a haven for low skills, low wages and low technologies, an ideological outpost of deregulated labour markets and enforced insecurities. Not only is that an impoverished vision for a great industrial, scientific and trading nation, but it will also not work. It is the wrong vision for the wrong arena. It is not the place where this country can find a secure economic future. The hysterical Conservative position on the minimum wage and the social chapter, contrary to the relaxed attitude of many leading businesses and in the face of agreed practice elsewhere, is a deliberate repudiation of a stakeholder approach. The attempt to put an 'Anglo-American' economic model into battle against a 'European' model is a distraction from the real task, in the new global economy, of building on what is most useful in both these models (and in others). We do not have to choose between dynamism and decency, flexibility and security: the sensible course is to find the right balance. Not only is this Labour's approach, but it reflects the best of business practice and the growing consensus of business theory. We have the prospect, perhaps for the first time ever, of a constructive partnership between all the stakeholders in the British economy directed towards agreed goals. This is one of the biggest prizes that this election can deliver.

SEVEN

A Responsible Society

Sometimes a chance remark says more than a shelf of worthy texts. The particular remark I have in mind came from a friend in the middle of a game of tennis. A GP, born in India, he had recently returned from a trip home to visit his elderly parents. When I asked how the visit had gone, he replied: 'I always come back thinking what life would have been like if I had been born on the other side of the road.' This 'other side of the road' question goes to the heart of political choice. What responsibility do we, and should we, have towards the other side of the road? What kind of societies are implied by the answers we give? Although it may get lost in the daily exchange of electoral missiles, this issue defines the choice of party and philosophy in this election. Labour's one-nation approach, with its emphasis on social cohesion and mutual responsibility, confronts a Conservative Party in the grip of an irresponsible creed of competitive individualism.

Of course, we do not know on which side of the road we shall be born (which is why some philosophers invite us to play the imaginary game of choosing the kind of society we would prefer to be born into on the basis of such ignorance). But what we do know is that we are all in some sense on the other side of the road – for example, when we are ill, old, disabled, without a job – at some point in our lives. More than that, we know that we all have to live in the same society and the same world: roads cross and meet. Labour's argument is that it is not only morally right to believe in shared responsibility and social inclusiveness, the kernel of an ethic of community, but that it makes sense for a society to organize itself as much as possible on this basis. A fractured and divided society is wrong, but it is also damaging to social and economic health.

The evidence for this is all around us. The growing numbers excluded from a common citizenship since 1979 – the rise from one in ten to one in three children living in households with income less than half the average, the doubling of the number of people dependent on benefits from one in twelve to one in six, one in five families now without anyone in employment – finds its expression in a society demoralized and damaged by the degradation of neighbourhoods, the weakening of families, the explosion of crime and the decline of civic order. At its simplest level, despite new opportunities and rising incomes, there is a widespread feeling that Britain has become a less pleasant place in which to live. Far from a 'rising tide lifting all boats', the original promise of New Right Conservatism in the 1980s, the tide of poverty, inequality and exclusion threatens to sink the ship. It is not surprising that there is now growing research evidence, not just from Britain but from around the world, that provides dismal confirmation of what should have been elementary truths. The central truth is that divided societies are weak and cohesive societies are strong.

Thus a recent report from the traditionally free-market Organization for Economic Cooperation and Development (OECD) was forced to conclude that those societies, notably the United States and the United Kingdom, which had most rigorously followed its prescriptions were the societies where income and wage inequality had widened most sharply, with the associated problems of poverty and social exclusion. Nor had greater inequality produced more growth or employment for the United Kingdom, contrary to the promise of the New Conservatives. By contrast, those societies of east Asia which had experienced the most dramatic growth were marked by increasing income equality and intensive social investment in education and skills. Richard Wilkinson (whose recent book *Unhealthy Societies: The Afflictions of Inequality* pulls together the new evidence) summarizes what we now know: 'First, that increases in social cohesion, which we all regard as desirable, are largely dependent on reducing the size of income differences. Second, that narrower income differences and increased social cohesion play a very powerful role in reducing not only violent crime, but also national death rates from some of the most important diseases. Third, regardless of what may have been true in the past, in modern economic life narrower income differences are associated with faster – not slower – economic growth.' What is extraordinary is that the lesson that we thought had been learned from the great reformers of the last century and this – that the route to greater national efficiency lay through an attack on poverty, insanitary conditions, poor housing, illiteracy, malnutrition and insecurity – should recently have been so comprehensively forgotten. Yet the Government's Health of the Nation programme did not even include a reduction in health inequality as one of its targets.

This cumulative evidence from the OECD and elsewhere on the effects of inequality and social exclusion has begun to force fresh thinking. One example is an interesting article in the *Financial Times* a few months ago by the paper's economics columnist, Martin Wolf ('The dilemma of inequality', 23 July 1996), in which he warns of the dangers to market economies if present trends are allowed to continue.

After pointing out that the development of the market economy was accompanied by a parallel development of democratic rights, trade union protection, welfare states and full employment, he issues a chilling warning about the consequences that will follow from the erosion of these supports: 'The US may be big enough to allow the rich to escape from the poor. That is far less feasible in more crowded countries.' Already there are dangerous politicians in evidence throughout the West who have identified the rich seam of despair and discontent to be exploited for an extremist politics of hatred and fear among people for whom the promises of democracy and the market economy are no longer conjoined. The zealots of the New Conservatism are not only morally wrong in their repudiation of a shared citizenship and the responsibilities that are attached to this, but they are further wrong in believing that a secure and successful market economy can be built on the basis of widening inequalities and social exclusion. Conversely, social cohesion and solidarity are not just morally right, but they are the foundation upon which successful societies and strong economies can flourish.

Here is one of the great fault lines in this election. There are radically different approaches on offer, expressed across the whole policy arena, which will take this society along sharply different paths and lead to quite different destinations. The moment has arrived when we have to decide whether we want to take social cohesion seriously or not, whether we want to proceed on the basis that we are members of one nation or on the basis that we are individual market players. One approach leads to stakeholding and shared responsibility; the other to a Hobbesian war of all against all. Both will have their consequences, but they will be very different consequences. In case this contrast and choice seem too sharply drawn, consider some of the policy areas where it is most clearly expressed.

Why Vote Labour?

Let us return for a moment to the 'other side of the road' question. Here the contrast is between an approach that is content to provide at best a few refugee routes from one side to the other and an approach that wants both to provide a mass transit system and to improve the general condition of the road. Any decent politics will concern itself with the lot of those who have least (the Conservative changes to the tax and benefit system, and the deliberate erosion of the state pension, have revealed an opposite concern), but it will also construct broad pathways to something better. Here Labour's emphasis on skilling and training, its welfare-into-work package and its strategies on youth and long-term unemployment make up a vigorous exercise in road-crossing. It is all about including and giving a stake, in ways that are beneficial both to the individuals themselves and to society at large.

Consider the issue of the minimum wage upon which so much Conservative electoral fire is directed. A minimum wage will not only enable hundreds of thousands of people to secure a floor against exploitation and an escape from benefit dependency (800,000 people currently earn less than £2.50 per hour, while in-work benefits cost every taxpayer £120 per year), but it is a direct expression of a politics of inclusion and social cohesion. It is also an argument that Labour has won. In the words of John Philpott, director of the independent Employment Policy Institute, 'a sober economic appraisal suggests that in the real world of complex labour markets, a sensible minimum wage would help considerable numbers of low-paid workers without causing untold economic harm'. Yet despite the careful way in which it will be introduced, at a level which will avoid adverse employment effects and through a consultative commission with business interests, New Conservative dogma still insists that a market economy should not acknowledge even this modest amount of economic and social responsibility. The argument about the European Social Chapter provision for works councils and the right to be represented by a trade union are of the same kind: a politics that seeks to include meets an assertion of market irresponsibility. Not only that, measures such as these which are seen as basic attributes of industrial citizenship elsewhere, across the political spectrum, are seen by the new breed of British Conservatives as outrageous regulatory burdens. There will be many consequences of viewing matters in this way, but a growth of social cohesion will not be among them. Similarly, in opposing the EU Parental Leave directive, designed to help 'the reconciliation of professional and family life', the Government makes a nonsense of its hand-wringing about the family, schools and social order.

Then there is education, where the refugee route represented by the current Assisted Places Scheme, which involves spending over £100 million of public money to send a selection of children to private schools, contrasts with Labour's intention to transfer that money to bringing primary-level class sizes down for all as part of a commitment to raise standards across the board. As the Conservative MP, George Walden, has forcefully argued, we already pay a terrible price for what he calls the educational and social 'apartheid' of a system in which the 7 per cent of children who attend private schools collect 80 per cent of the GCSE and A-level league table prizes and take nearly 50 per cent of the places at Oxford and Cambridge, and whose families (along with most Conservative MPs) have no stake in the schools attended by the children of the vast majority of the population. He proposes a state buy-out of a raft of these schools. Another idea (not Labour's, I should quickly add) would be to allow universities to recruit students only in proportion to the distribution of numbers in different types of school. Yet the task is not to destroy excellence, but to make it available to all. Here the public policy agenda has been staring us in the face for a generation, but we have resolutely dodged it. The Old Left dodged it because it thought it had done its job with the arrival of the comprehensive principle, forgetting that the real job came in making the practice live up to that founding principle of excellence for all; while the New Right has dodged it because it has preferred to fight structural and mechanical battles against ideological enemies. Not the least of New Labour's achievements has been to grasp the nettle of school improvement, even if this has meant taking the occasional sting.

It is the responsibility of parents to try to provide the most appropriate education for their children; it is the responsibility of public policy to provide a decent education for all. This means sustained investment, with those who need most getting most, but also a robust pedagogy (this morning on the radio I heard a distinguished professor of English Literature make the dotty claim that the decline of poetry in schools was caused by a lack of resources). The Conservatives seem content to publish league tables showing that schools which are academically or socially selective (or both) carry off all the prizes. Yet this is as absurd as allowing some doctors to select only healthy patients for their lists and then producing league tables of patient health purporting to show that these were the most successful doctors because their patients topped the tables. Information can illuminate issues; but only if it is good information (which raw league tables are not) and only if public policy then tackles those issues seriously and vigorously. Selection (or 'differentiation' in the jargon) should be basic to education: teachers (like doctors) should treat different needs in different ways. But it is only the Conservatives who think this pedagogical truism is incompatible with social cohesion. What we should be obsessed with is why similar schools can perform in markedly dissimilar ways and then put tough strategies in place to universalize best practice. This is now the central thrust of Labour's approach (which I would like to take even further with a primary-leaving certificate demonstrating proven competence in basic literacy and numeracy, to be retaken thereafter if not achieved then) and is the only approach that takes excellence for all seriously.

A further – and crucial – area in which the choice made in this election will shape all our futures is welfare and social policy. There may seem to be broad agreement that 'something must be done about welfare', but this disguises fundamentally different approaches. The growth in social security spending has been dramatic: it accounted for one sixth of total spending when the post-war Labour Government left office, now it accounts for one third. New demands and needs press in all the time (for example, there are now nearly one million people in England and Wales over eighty-five, a 17 per cent increase between 1991 and 1995 alone, and the United Kingdom as a whole will see a 43.6 per cent increase in the over-sixty population by 2025). The Conservative approach has been to attack claimant groups such as lone parents, despite official research showing that 77 per cent of lone parents reported that it was the lack of child care that was trapping them on benefit, and to cut into entitlements (as with the breaking of the earnings link in the state pension, shrinking it from 21 per cent of average male earnings in 1979 to 14 per cent today, producing the scandal of mass pensioner poverty). The first choice is to decide whether we are prepared to regard the welfare issue in terms of cutting collective provision or recasting collective provision in new ways. The former approach is that of the Conservatives; the latter is Labour's. The welfare state is only unaffordable if we decide not to afford it. Choice should not be disguised as necessity.

Why Vote Labour?

As we look ahead, the contrasting nature of the different approaches stands out clearly. Not content with merely trying to contain the rate of increase of the current welfare budget, the New Conservative Right will seek to privatize as much and as far as possible, retaining only what it likes to call a 'safety net' for the poor. This will be an explicit rejection of any notion of social inclusion in the matter of welfare. Rich and poor will inhabit different universes of provision (and, as Richard Titmuss once remarked, services that are only for the poor always end up being poor services). The way in which millions of people were bribed by the Conservative Government to leave occupational or state pension schemes and take out private pensions – on such bad advice and losing as much as a quarter of their contributions in fees and commissions that over a million people are still awaiting compensation – is just the most glaring illustration of where this road leads. The alternative approach is for the state to guarantee a bedrock of common provision (within and beyond which individuals can make their own arrangements) in the key areas of welfare such as pensions and continuing care. As individuals and as a society, the stark truth is that we need to spend more on welfare not less. Unless we are prepared for radical market solutions, of the kind described above, we shall need to explore radical collective solutions. This does not necessarily mean direct state provision, which may be neither possible nor desirable, but it does mean that an intelligent state accepts responsibility for ensuring that universal insurance provision is made. This could be through a reinvented national insurance system or through new comprehensive 'stakeholder' schemes (or a mixture of both), with the state and the private sector working in partnership to establish inclusive schemes with a clear framework of responsibility, return and regulation. The New Conservative Right may describe this as compulsion, as it does with taxation; but everybody else will recognize it as a sensible expression of shared responsibility and social inclusiveness. Experience also suggests that it makes administrative and economic sense. Much of the argument in this area can seem hopelessly complex and technical, but this should not obscure the fact that the central issue is one of principle and philosophy. The sorts of pension we shall have, or the kind of continuing care we shall receive, will depend upon the choices we make now.

The whole issue of responsibility lies at the heart of politics today. A responsible society is one in which both the state and its citizens discharge their respective responsibilities and in which there is a reciprocity of relationship around common ends. There is, of course, political disagreement around each component of this statement; and there is a real sense in which the neo-liberal conservatism of the New Right, in explicitly rejecting a public purpose distinct from market outcomes, is a doctrine of irresponsibility. But that need not prevent those of us who want to live in a responsible society from trying to put one together. It requires a social responsibility from the state, in doing all it can to prevent social exclusion and an underclass of the dispossessed and alienated. It requires an economic responsibility, to promote work, wealth and opportunity. And it requires a political responsibility, of those who govern to those who are governed.

It also requires a clear environmental responsibility, to tackle the inescapable problems of environmental degradation and unsustainable growth which threaten everyone's quality of life now as well as the welfare of future generations. The fact is that only radical, strategically intelligent government can deliver the environmental goods – economic instruments such as 'green taxes' are not enough alone, and sometimes penalize the most vulnerable in society. The New Conservatives' obsession with the 'untrammelled' free market makes it ultimately impossible for the few genuinely green souls in their party to do what we all know has to be done. We desperately need to develop fewer car-dependent transport policies, to promote energy efficiency and green technologies, to set and enforce ambitious limits to pollution and heavy penalties for those who overstep the mark. Labour is committed to a fully integrated and strategic approach to the environment in government and will set up new and powerful cross-departmental bodies to help develop policy and audit environmental performance. A Labour government would put a high priority not only on responsible stewardship of our corner of the planet, but also on being leaders in the world on environmental issues. On each of these counts, and on all of them cumulatively, this election offers a choice between responsibility and irresponsibility.

But a state that accepts its own responsibility is also entitled to ask and expect reciprocal responsibility from its citizens. Indeed it could be said that a state is *only* entitled to ask and expect this if it is discharging its part of the responsibility contract with its citizens. This kind of reciprocity distinguishes Labour's approach, explicitly or implicitly, on a range of fronts. Its commitment to provide work or training to unemployed young people does not carry a non-participation option. Receipt of benefits is linked to the obligation to develop strategies for work. A minimum wage to protect some workers against exploitation requires other groups of workers not to use it to shift differentials across the board. Support for business demands responsibility in the boardroom. Enjoying the benefits of public spending means paying fair taxes. Investment in nursery and school provision requires parents to fulfil their part of the educational contract. A commitment to decent housing provision means that anti-social tenants are required not to make life a misery for neighbours and estates. Environmental action by government has to be matched by appropriate behaviour from consumers. Such obligations – to be good parents, workers, employers, neighbours, citizens – already exist and do not derive from government; but a government that is actively discharging its own responsibilities in these matters is clearly better able to ask others to discharge theirs.

This is manifestly so in relation to crime. In terms of responsibility, the maintenance of order is a core state responsibility (and the condition for the state's own continued existence). The Conservative failure in this area is now official: despite having record numbers in prison, at vast cost, the crime rate has doubled and is again rising. There is a terrible inevitability about this. A policy devised to win plaudits at Conservative Party conferences has done nothing to stop the cancer of crime that ruins lives, breeds fear and destroys communities. An argument conducted in terms of being 'soft' or 'hard' on crime has obscured the real choice between being intelligent or stupid. It is stupid to pretend that social conditions do not breed crime ('you only have to look at the dock in a Crown Court to see who is there' in the words of Judge Stephen Tumim, former Chief Inspector of Prisons) or that prevention and deterrence are not more effective than simply building more crime-promoting prisons. A responsible state will be energetic on *all* fronts – social and economic strategies to tackle the roots of crime, concerted action on prevention, an effective range of punishments and therapies – and not invent bogus alternatives. The robust punishment of wickedness needs always to go hand in hand with the strenuous cultivation of virtue. The former is of course easier; but the latter is more fundamental. Ever longer sentences and ever more prisons may dominate the political agenda of a failed Home Secretary about to face the wrath of the electorate; but making sure that there is a family adviser and a family education support centre attached

to every deprived school (to take just one example) is likely
to do more to make us a more secure society in the long run.
We know that 26 per cent of prisoners have been in care as
children, just as we know that three quarters of all offenders
come from the poorest section of the population. This should
be enough to persuade an intelligent government that the
best way to tackle crime is to attack the epicentres of social
breakdown in deprived neighbourhoods, distressed families,
sink schools and broken communities. Rebuilding the social
capital of such areas offers more durable security for all of
us than building ever more prisons. It is also right. If Labour
has developed tough new policies to deal with criminals,
including fast-track punishment for persistent young
offenders and action on vandalism and anti-social behaviour
in neighbourhoods, it is because it is discharging the full
range of its other responsibilities. By contrast, Conservative
policies that promote crime on one hand while lamenting its
consequences on the other exhibit an irresponsibility that
guarantees failure.

Some people may feel uneasy about Labour's emphasis on
community and responsibility, thinking that at best it is
irrelevantly nostalgic and at worst dangerously authori-
tarian. If understood properly, it is neither. It does not deny
the importance of experiment and diversity, or the fact that
the community is made up of a plurality of communities,
nor does it involve the state poking around in people's private
lives where it has no business. But it does involve a challenge
both to the possessive individualism of the New Right and
to the thin rights-based liberalism of some of the Old Left:
neither can provide the basis for a new politics of community
and responsibility that redraws the balance between rights
and duties, individual purposes and shared purposes, me and
we. It is a measure of the extent to which we have lost sight
of what we once knew that the attempt to renegotiate this

balance on various fronts should provoke such antipathy in some quarters. Whatever else we may suffer from, it is not an excess of community or responsibility. The attempt to remedy this deficiency — in families, in the streets, on the roads, in businesses, on television screens, in our schools — forces us to define what kind of society we are and what kind of society we want to be. If we reject this enterprise, or have no response to it, then we really are in trouble. No warm-glow rhetoric about social cohesion will for long conceal the absence of a social purpose. Perhaps this election may even prove to be the moment when we find one.

EIGHT

A New Democracy

I think back to that memorable and moving day last July, when Nelson Mandela addressed both Houses of Parliament in the history-heavy setting of Westminster Hall, where in the thirteenth century King Henry III had been made to swear an oath that he would respect Magna Carta and the rights of citizens. Now here was a man who has spent more than a third of his life in prison arriving as the President of the new democracy of South Africa and telling us, softly and simply, what he had learned from the past and what he hoped for the future. His rancour-free gentleness even invited us to overlook the hypocrisy that some of those Conservative personages now welcoming him had once been the apologists for the apartheid system that had imprisoned him.

For me there was one sentence in particular in what Nelson Mandela said on that day that stood out. It seemed to hang in the air, an unsettling challenge to the stately surroundings and the constitutional complacencies. Having described his new country's commitment to a democratic political system, he added: 'Within that broad framework, like other nations, we continue to struggle to find ways and means by which to involve the citizen as intimately as possible in the system of government, cognizant of the historical process which is redefining the role of the politician, taking away from these professions the powers conferred by the notion that they, exclusively, have a special ability to govern.' This was a striking message for a new democracy to deliver to an old one, in such a setting, on such an occasion, and to such an assembly of professional politicians. It challenges us to think of democracy not merely as an achievement of the past but as an active and continuing project for the present. It is a challenge to do politics differently.

Its relevance to this country and to this election is direct and immediate. The outcome of this election will decide whether our political system is reformed and modernized ('a new politics for a new century' as the late John Smith liked to describe it), or whether we shall continue to muddle along – or at least to try to – in the same old way. The contrast between Labour and the Conservatives on this could not be sharper: a bold programme of political reform versus a sterile adherence to a failing and discredited system, an attempt to develop a new kind of politics versus a belief that some people have 'a special ability to govern' as Mandela described it. Perhaps the clearest and most astonishing example of the contrast is the fact that the Conservative Party enters an election on the eve of the twenty-first century defending the voting rights of hereditary peers in an unreformed House of Lords. If such an elementary democratic outrage is acceptable to them, it is not surprising that the rest of the democratic agenda is an alien land as far as the Conservatives are concerned.

Such a position is not merely wrong, it is also stupid. Here the case of Scotland (and Wales, if less urgently) makes the point. It is apparent for all to see that the people of Scotland want a parliament (a preference that Labour will rightly enable them to confirm in a referendum), yet the Conservatives propose to deny them both a parliament and a referendum. The stupidity of this position for an avowedly unionist party is that it could destroy the union. This was perfectly clear to a previous and wiser generation of Conservative politicians (such as Edward Heath and Sir Alec Douglas-Home), which is why they proposed schemes of devolution, but even such obvious statecraft eludes the current crop of visionless Conservatives. They share with narrow nationalists a responsibility for fanning the flames of separatism. Those of us who value the union of this kingdom of several nations, both for what it has achieved in the past and for what it can achieve in the future, want to reform the union in order to preserve it. This conservative principle has been forgotten, or abandoned, by the New Conservatives. There are certainly important matters of large detail still to be resolved, but the central choice now is between centralism and decentralism, remaking the union or breaking it, sense and stupidity.

What is not surprising is that the long Conservative period of power since 1979 has coincided with a growing interest in issues of political and constitutional reform. All the survey evidence points to mounting public disaffection with the political process (and with politicians) and strong support for a raft of radical reforms. So ruthless and shameless has been the Conservative exploitation of a political system which gives too much power to governments and too little power to those who should control them, involving an alarming absence of proper checks and balances, that the essential nature of this system has been exposed in all its unreformed nakedness. So what has been exposed? An electoral system that allows a minority to pretend to be a majority. A House of Commons rendered supine by party and patronage (over 130 Conservative MPs have been given knighthoods since 1979 and the 'payroll' vote inflated by the barrel-scraping proliferation of the ludicrously over-titled Parliamentary Private Secretaries to even the lowest forms of ministerial life) and incapable of holding the executive to effective account. A lack of protection for citizen rights that has forced Britons to be the most frequent visitors to Strasbourg in search of a justice that they were denied at home (resulting in more than thirty judgements against the Conservative Government, with a recent study finding Britain to be in breach of over forty of the international human rights obligations that it has signed up to). An unreformed second chamber that can be packed when necessary with hereditary Conservative peers. A doctrine of parliamentary sovereignty that can be deployed to snuff out intermediate institutions or remake them in the image of the regime. A culture of secrecy that prevents the free flow of information that is the lifeblood of an effective democracy.

The Conservatives did not invent these features of the British way of politics; but what they have done since 1979 is to exploit them to the full. Bad legislation (from the poll tax to private pensions, child support to dangerous dogs) has been whipped through a compliant Commons with inadequate consultation and ineffective scrutiny. Ministers have resigned when discovered in the wrong bed but not when responsible for the wrong policies. A remorseless process of centralization (what Simon Jenkins calls 'the Tory nationalization of Britain') has undermined local government and put ever more powers into the hands of ministers. The vast edifice of the quango state has been assembled, now accounting for over one third of total central government expenditure and staffed by at least 66,000 unelected, unknown and unaccountable quangocrats. The National Health Service has been reorganized in a way that has removed it from any form of local community control (for example, the public does not even have the right to attend meetings of NHS Trusts). Government departments have been broken up into executive agencies, but with no clear lines of political accountability (agency heads have rolled to save ministerial scalps, as with the Child Support Agency and the Prison Service), while other functions have been farmed out to the private sector. What all this shows is that the Conservatives have certainly been interested in constitutional change; but their revolution in government has exploited the opportunities offered by a system of unchecked power. The reinvention of government has not been accompanied by the reinvention of accountability.

Here it is a case of a New Conservatism kicking over the traces of an older Conservative tradition. That older tradition of 'little platoons', concerned to defend local and intermediate institutions against what it regarded as state centralism, has been replaced by the New Conservatism of centralist authoritarianism. This has sought to justify itself by claiming that it has invented a 'consumer' democracy that is more efficient than elective democracy (as William Waldegrave once expressed it: 'the key point is not whether those who run our public services are elected, but whether they are producer-responsive or consumer-responsive'). This cheerful abandonment of elective accountability has produced a situation in which we are floating on a sea of 'charters' but where nobody is responsible for anything any more. Legitimacy is eroded, democracy is weakened, and politics itself is shown the door. Yet the truth is surely that we want better forms of political democracy *and* better forms of consumer democracy, not as false opposites but as part of the continuing attempt to develop a more self-governing society.

Two judges, Nolan and Scott, have recently done more than anyone else to illuminate the nature of government in Britain and the particular nature of Conservative government. Although John Major likes to claim credit for calling them in, the inquiries undertaken by these judges (cash-for-questions and associated sleaze in the case of Nolan, arms-to-Iraq with Scott) were the forced responses of a Government in the political mire. The Government's evidence to Nolan on quangos and the patronage state amounted to a bland assurance that all was well in the best of all possible worlds; Nolan repudiated such nonsense and proposed a raft of reforms to improve accountability. But Nolan's careful exposure of the extent to which Members of Parliament (overwhelmingly Conservative ones) were on the payroll of outside interests was even more devastating. Those Tory MPs who had taken money for asking parliamentary questions were simply the tip of an enormous iceberg of interests. As Lord Nolan's report described it: 'In recent years Members have acquired paid consultancies on a large scale. Over the same period public scepticism about MPs' financial motives has increased sharply. It must be more likely than not that these two developments are related, but in any case their combination can only tend to undermine the dignity of Parliament as a whole.'

But what was also documented was the consistent failure of the club culture of the House of Commons over many years to regulate the conduct of its members. In Nolan's masterly understatement: 'The overall picture is not one of an institution whose Members have been quick to recognize or respond to public concern.' Even so, in November 1995 over 270 Conservative MPs still voted to keep their outside earnings secret despite the recommendations of Lord Nolan, while the Government has consistently refused to allow Nolan to look into the murky world of party funding. Not only that, but a Government whip was found trying to stitch up the Committee concerned with investigating the latest and most notorious cash-for-questions case. Whatever else they have done, the New Conservatives have brought the language and practice of sleaze to British politics and in doing so have done great damage to politics, politicians and to Parliament itself.

The voluminous report by Sir Richard Scott tells a similar story. It shows a Government deliberately and consistently misleading Parliament in order to avoid political embarrassment. In case this is thought to be a partial description, consider the summary given by Sir Richard (to me, as it happens) in a Commons Select Committee last year:

Q. Did something constitutionally improper happen?
A. Yes, I think it did and I said so.

Q. Did ministers behave in ways that ministers ought constitutionally not to have behaved?
A. I have said so, yes.

Q. Was Parliament denied information that Parliament constitutionally ought to have been provided with?
A. I think so, yes.

And the Government's response to Scott's verdict that it had misled Parliament, concealed what ought to have been revealed and conducted itself in a constitutionally improper manner? The most blatant and brazen operation, supported by the massed ranks of the congenitally craven parliamentary Conservative Party, to traduce Scott, distort his findings and evade responsibility. It was a breathtaking example of the arrogance of power and a mockery of ministerial responsibility to Parliament. When the history of the period is written, this episode will surely be seen as the nadir of an unreformed politics.

What Labour is now offering is an ambitious programme of sustained reform of this unreformed system. Just to sketch some of its leading elements is to see the scale and range of what is proposed. The removal of the voting rights of hereditary peers will begin the process of creating a modern second chamber. Long-overdue changes in the way the Commons works will make it less of a party pantomime and more of an effective instrument for scrutinizing legislation and holding governments to account. New rules on the funding of political parties will make the system more open and honest. Building on Nolan, clearer and firmer provisions on the conduct and interests of Members of Parliament will begin to restore the reputation of Parliament (and perhaps even of politicians). The quango state will be brought to democratic heel, with measures to increase accountability and control patronage appointments. A referendum on the voting system will give people a chance to reject a system that props up a winner-takes-all kind of politics in favour of one that increases political choice and makes all votes count (or, of course, not to reject such a system). Local government will be renewed and its civic role strengthened, including an elected authority for London and with innovations such as directly elected mayors. Scotland and Wales will acquire more control over their own affairs, while regions in England will be strengthened in relation to central government. The protection of basic human rights will be enhanced with the incorporation of the European Convention on Human Rights into our domestic law, a prelude to the development of a Bill of Rights of our own. The notorious secrecy of government in Britain will be transformed by a Freedom of Information Act of the kind that is standard elsewhere, a recognition that information is not to be regarded as a grant from government (as in the Conservative Government's 'code of practice') but as a fundamental right of citizenship.

This is a bold and daunting programme of political reform, to which the monarchy should be added too, but it is also massively overdue. It should be seen not as a shopping list of separate items but as an interlocking and coherent process of political renewal. Just as the irresponsible nature of the British political system accurately reflects a wider economic and social irresponsibility, the development of a stakeholder democracy is an integral part of the wider reform process in society and the economy. Similarly, when Labour proposes an independent food standards agency, or a guaranteed independence for the government's statistical service, or a new environmental audit committee to monitor progress on CO_2 emissions reduction and other environmental objectives, this represents an assertion of a public interest in these matters that is poorly protected in an executive-dominated political system without secure accountabilities. We have paid a very high price for failing to make our political system work better, either because we were in the grip of attitudes that prevented us from understanding what had to be done or because we allowed particular reform initiatives to be derailed by constitutional conservatives (in both parties). It is true that Labour was slower in its embrace of constitutional radicalism than some of us would have liked; but this makes it all the more significant that it has adopted such a radical programme now. While the Conservatives tinker around the edges of a failed status quo, Labour wants to revitalize parliamentary democracy and civic life. There have been great reform waves in the past that have moved our political system along in more democratic directions – extending the suffrage, votes for women, outlawing corrupt practices, strengthening Parliament – and it is time for another great wave of reform now. As the party that opposed so many democratic reforms in the past, perhaps it is not surprising that the Conservatives are to be found opposing them this time too. Not for the first time, history will have to move on without them and wait for them, eventually, to catch up.

People are rightly disgusted by the way in which some Conservative MPs are found to be in the pay of lobbyists, and the way in which the Conservative machine tried to fix the process by which the House of Commons is supposed to investigate such matters, but this disgust needs to be extended to the cosy and clubby system of ineffective self-regulation that has been allowed to hold sway for so long. In a constitution that is made up as we go along, we have failed to develop the machinery for guarding and developing it, while reform initiatives have been sporadic, piecemeal and frequently ill-fated. We invent ad hoc responses (such as the Nolan Committee) when crises press in, but neglect the need for durable constitutional machinery. This is why I hope that Labour will convert Nolan into a permanent Constitutional Commission, with new membership and status, in order that the whole range of constitutional issues can be given a more secure, informed and dynamic basis than has been the case in the past.

But if political reform is seen as no more than a process of institutional change, however radical and coherent, the real nature of the political opportunities now becoming available will be missed. For what this election promises is not merely a new constitution, but a new kind of politics in Britain. Tony Blair in particular seems to want this; while the civil war inside the Conservative Party opens up the prospect of seismic changes in the political landscape. There is a radical disjuncture between the traditional yah-boo adversarialism that distinguishes politics in Britain, the currency of which is iron certainties, polar opposites and rival simplicities, and the kind of politics that is appropriate for a world in which old ideological paradigms have collapsed, cleavages and allegiances become more fluid, and where uncertainty stalks the globe. We need a kind of politics that is about learning, pluralism and cooperation; what we have had is a kind of trench warfare in which the sole object has been to decapitate opponents. This is not a plea to take the politics out of politics; but it is a plea for a more useful and engaging kind of politics than we have practised in Britain for many decades past.

The Conservatives since 1979, in deliberately repudiating consensus and agreement, have made matters much worse. Mrs Thatcher's early abandonment of the tradition of Royal Commissions on major issues came to symbolize the partisan arrogance of the New Conservatives. Yet it is simply not sensible to convert every issue into partisan form, forcing them into the grinding mill of party strife, and the effect of doing so is to prevent sustained agreement in policy areas where such agreement is badly needed. On a range of important matters – for example, pensions, continuing care of the elderly, higher education, nursery provision, environmental protection, constitutional reform – much unnecessary damage is done by our routinized yah-booism. Organizing the entire proceedings of the House of Commons on this basis is a disaster; while conducting political argument in the same way is a dispiriting turn-off for the public. We badly need a more grown-up kind of politics in Britain and one of the most refreshing things about Tony Blair is that he genuinely seems to want to supply it.

It may be that only a different kind of electoral system can really produce a different kind of politics, but this does not prevent progress being made now. Labour's deliberate refusal to make the Northern Ireland question a matter of party politics has rightly been seen as both commendable and useful. The cross-party Scottish Convention has been a remarkable exercise in the politics of agreement on constitutional issues, with many lessons for the rest of Britain both in terms of the process and the product. The prospect of cooperation between Labour and the Liberal Democrats, already commonplace in local government, is only anathema to those so conditioned by the British model of arid adversarialism that they cannot imagine a kind of pluralistic politics in which it is possible for parties to compete vigorously *and* cooperate constructively. This is the moment of truth for the Liberal Democrats in particular: having preached the virtues of a more cooperative kind of politics for so long, they now have to decide if they are serious about practising it. The omens are beginning to look more promising.

Instead of a stultifying and suffocating politics which pretends that all issues can be compressed into neat party boxes, with professional politicians claiming unique custody of the political process and genuine debate subordinated to the requirements of sound bite and spin, we would do well to take up Nelson Mandela's challenge to do politics differently. Labour's interest in new ways to involve people in decisions (such as citizens' juries) is a step in the right direction, as is its commitment to use the referendum to ensure that constitutional changes are rooted in popular assent. In a world in which technology offers new democratic opportunities, and in which many people are increasingly engaged in an issue politics beyond the parameters of conventional political choice, we need to think our way through to new institutions, instruments, styles and cultures appropriate to this new world. At least New Labour, in sharp contrast to the Conservatives, is in touch and in tune with this world. Its programme of political reform will modernize Britain's constitution. It will also herald a new kind of politics. And last but not least, it will make the currently polluted political air in Britain – the most disgraceful and damaging part of the Conservative legacy – refreshingly cleaner and sweeter.

NINE

Ourselves and Others

Who are we? And, being who we are, what do we want to do in the world? Such large questions may seem a million miles away from the fizz and spit of a general election campaign, but in fact they are right at the centre of this particular election. For this really is an election about who we are and where we want to go. Of all the alternatives and choices at issue now, this stands out as one of the most fundamental. The direction that is chosen now will define the kind of country we are, and the role we shall play in Europe and the world, for many years to come. It is an election about identity and vision.

Of course the identity of 'we' has always been a problem, as the linguistic elisions between 'England', 'Britain', 'Great Britain' and the 'United Kingdom' testify. It is not just the French who have trouble knowing whether we are *Angleterre*, *Grande Bretagne* or *Royaume-Uni*. Only globe-trotting business people confidently proclaim their membership of something called the UK (or even, horror of horrors, 'UK plc'). The inhabitants of England routinely forget that they are only the largest part of a multinational kingdom, sometimes quickly correcting 'England' to 'Britain' when they remember. The only authentic 'Britons' have often seemed to be the non-English inhabitants of these islands. Identity matters and crucially so, as a glance around the world shows; and it matters in a particular way to us. We have to sort out who we are, both here and in the wider world. With luck, the twin issues of devolution and Europe should enable us to do both. If so, it will make for a more relaxed and comfortable country in which to live. But if not, the current anguish and torment will be merely a foretaste of much worse to come.

In a recent article the writer Neal Ascherson recalled how schoolchildren used to describe themselves (do they still?) in the front of exercise books. In my own Middle England case, after my name, I would always describe where I lived in such terms as 'Desborough, Kettering, Northamptonshire, England, Britain, Europe, the World, the Galaxy, the Universe . . .' What this reminds us is that identities overlap, naturally and properly, some nearer and more intimate than others but all part of a process of adding on rather than subtracting or excluding. Or at least that is how it should be. The trouble is that a large and growing section of the Conservative Party is in the grip of a xenophobic nationalism, reducing Great Britain to a narrow and introverted Little England, disabling this country as an effective participant in decisions that will impact upon everyone who lives here and destined to make it a nastier and more unpleasant place. Just look at the flag-waving, feet-stamping, foreigner-bashing hordes now running rampant inside the Conservative Party, the respectable version of the lager-lubricated, Union Jack boxer-shorted militia of the football terraces, and ask yourself if that is a vision of the country in which anybody would like to live.

It is not surprising that civilized and intelligent Conservatives recoil from what they see happening to their party and, because of this, to their country. Thus Lord Howe, former Chancellor and Foreign Secretary, writing in the *Financial Times* (30 January 1995):

Why Vote Labour?

'Britain seems increasingly reconciled to an opt-out mentality, which foresees a future increasingly detached from Germany, France and the European mainstream. Rather than defining common interests and solutions with Bonn and Paris, the UK is expected to leave it to them to shape their future, and decide later whether to join arrangements which it has played no significant part in moulding. This is a profoundly negative prospect, humiliating to a great nation that aspires to world influence . . .'

Similarly, a clutch of former Conservative Foreign Secretaries and a former Prime Minister felt obliged to write a public letter (*Independent*, 19 September 1996) to their party pointing out that 'our greatest patriots have never been Little Englanders' and accusing those who were prepared to 'betray our national interest'.

Conservatives have always confused patriotism with jingoism, of course, and deliberately so. From the beginning of time the stock-in-trade of Conservative propaganda has been to wrap themselves shamelessly in the symbols of nationhood and to attack the patriotic credentials of their opponents, whether Liberal in the last century or Labour in this. As a classic academic study of the Conservative Party put it: 'Few democratic political parties can have so systematically and ruthlessly called into question the integrity, the devotion to the institutions of the country, and the patriotism of its opponents' (McKenzie and Silver, *Angels in Marble*, 1968). This is not a pretty or a principled politics, but it has proved alarmingly effective. Stomachs might turn, but votes have rolled in. When backs are against the political wall, as now, even fastidious Conservatives turn instinctively to this kind of jingoid armoury. Consider the recent pamphlet, *Blair's Gurus*, by the Conservative MP David Willetts, which makes some sensible and many silly points about the distinguished thinkers and writers who have influenced New Labour before announcing this conclusion: 'It is a desire not to be British which drives their agenda . . . It is because the Conservative Party represents this Britishness that they recognize that we are their implacable opponents.' It would be nice to think that he was as embarrassed writing such pathetic nonsense as the rest of us are in reading it.

As it happens, some of the best expressions of a proper patriotism and love of country have come from socialists. We might think of the essays of Orwell or, my own favourite, this passage from William Morris:

'The land is a little land; too much shut up within the narrow seas, as it seems, to have much space for swelling into hugeness: there are no great wastes overwhelming in their dreariness, no great solitudes of forests, no terrible untrodden mountain-walls: all is measured, mingled, varied, gliding easily one thing into another: little rivers, little plains, swelling, speedily-changing uplands, all beset with handsome orderly trees; little hills, little mountains, netted over with the walls of sheep-walks: all is little; yet not foolish and blank, but serious rather and abundant of meaning for such as choose to seek it: it is neither prison nor palace, but a decent home.'

Perhaps too pastoral, too English, too Cotswoldy even, but this is a love of country that does not feel the need to strut around parading its patriotic credentials nor to convert itself into a dangerous and damaging xenophobia. Not only this, but while the public school generals were blithely sending millions to reckless slaughter in the First World War trenches, or sections of the Tory establishment (and press) were busy appeasing Hitler and flirting with fascism in the 1930s, or when today's money abandons country in pursuit of tax-free irresponsibility, the ordinary people of this country have quietly attached themselves to the patriotism of the 'decent home'. This was a home to be defended ferociously when necessary, but not a base from which to attack the homes of others. British socialism and the British labour movement, rooted in a domestic world of collective self-help and an ethic of community, have better claim than most to represent this proper patriotism.

It would not be necessary to say any of this if the Conservatives had not decided that playing the jingo card on Europe, attacking the foreigners of 'Brussels' and Labour's alleged 'softness' towards such foreigners, would serve a useful political purpose in this election. The issue of the single currency provides the occasion and the opportunity to wheel out the old nationalist kitbag. Some Conservatives may hold their noses and shuffle their feet, or even try forlornly to hold the line, but the party's simmering civil war on Europe means that getting through the election before the party blows itself to pieces becomes the only imperative. This would perhaps not matter except for the fact that the Conservatives are in government; and that Britain is therefore utterly disabled in shaping the Europe that is now being made. On a recent visit to Sweden, one of Britain's natural allies on a range of European issues, I found Swedish politicians of all parties shaking their heads in disbelief and dismay at an approach to Europe that consists only of sending officials and ministers to Brussels to 'block for Britain'.

In this election we are called upon to demonstrate whether we understand that being British means being European too. Only then can we play our full and proper part in deciding the kind of Europe we want to build. It is a moment for fundamental choice. Those who say that the European Union is neither fully European nor really a union are right, but it is the best that the continent has achieved so far. In the words of Timothy Garton Ash, 'the EU is the worst possible

"Europe", apart from all the other Europes that have been tried from time to time'. It is difficult to know where the Conservative Europhobes have been during this twentieth century. We may despair at the protectionist lunacies of the Common Agricultural Policy or rumoured regulations about the size of Cox's apples, but the much greater lunacy is not to understand that a Europe of institutional cooperation is better than the kind of Europe that has seen the continent and its peoples devastated twice in this century. Not to understand this is not to understand anything. And not to understand it in the name of a bogus patriotism is the real betrayal.

When Chancellor Kohl expresses his fears for a Germany outside Europe, the sensible reaction is not one of Germanophobe outrage but respect and support for his determination to lock Germany into a wider European structure. When France and Germany work closely together on European issues, the proper response is not to mutter churlishly from the sidelines but to rejoice in the partnership and to join them on the field. Those Conservatives who like to excite each other with notions of Britain 'pulling out of Europe' display a reckless disregard for this country's political and economic interests. It is not just that 60 per cent of our trade is with Europe, or that the inward investment that the Conservatives like to proclaim as their great economic achievement would be stopped in its tracks by withdrawal, but that Britain belongs in Europe. We are a great European nation and we need to start acting like one.

This does not mean signing up to the wilder flights of integrationist fancy of some enthusiasts for the European project. Contrary to how these issues are usually presented, the world is not peopled exclusively by Europhobes or Europhiles. Most people (and even most politicians, if only this majority could assert itself) are Euro-realists. They know that Britain belongs in Europe, but they want a kind of Europe that they feel comfortable with. The tragedy is that the nature of this Europe is being decided now and will be decided in the years immediately ahead and that Britain under the Conservatives, where the European issue has become wholly a matter of internal party management, is currently unable to contribute positively to this process. We have been relegated to the negative role of petulant irritants, when we should be articulating a positive vision of the kind of Europe we want to see and winning allies for this vision. The election of a Labour Government is not merely desirable for this, but an absolute precondition.

Europe is badly in need of a new vision. The Maastricht ratification process, with all its manifest difficulties, should have alerted European political leaders and the technocrats of Brussels to the fact that without a renewed popular basis for the European project it would wither on the vine. A 'people's Europe' is not a slogan but a necessity. This, by the way, is why a 'social' Europe as represented by the Social Chapter is a necessary component of the European enterprise. There is room for argument about the extent of its provisions, but not about the fact that a Europe that defines itself only as a single market will fail to excite the imagination or command the allegiance of its people. Unfortunately, Maastricht did not prompt the stocktaking that was conspicuously needed. Indeed, it can be argued that, in devoting its energies to the advancement of economic and monetary union (EMU) at the expense of almost everything else, Europe failed to rise to the challenge of the two great issues it was faced with: enlargement and unemployment. Both have to be central to a new vision. The post-Communist opportunity to bring the countries of eastern and central Europe into the European mainstream is a historic obligation of supreme importance. The need to make the attack on unemployment central to European efforts (with the OECD predicting that 18.8 million EU citizens will be without jobs at the end of 1996, and scarcely 70 per cent of men of working age in work) should be too obvious to state. This is why Labour will support the Swedish proposal to write an employment objective into the European treaty.

It is difficult to avoid the conclusion that the imperative of EMU has made these other objectives more difficult to achieve (and may continue to do so). But the fact is that the single currency is the part of the European project that is currently on the table, whether we would like it to be or not. In this situation neither reckless embrace in an orgy of Euro-enthusiasm nor reckless repudiation in a fit of Euro-pique makes sense as far as British interests are concerned. There may be long-term advantages in terms of growth and stability in having a single currency, but these are uncertain and there may be shorter-term costs as well as the loss of domestic adjustment capability. There is a case for Britain being a first-wave entrant, in terms of securing its position and avoiding interest-rate premiums that may have to be paid for being a non-Euro currency, but much will depend on the precise relationship between the 'ins' and the 'outs'. There is also a case for regarding EMU as a misconceived project which, if founded on bogus convergence criteria, may in fact prove damaging and even dangerous to the larger European project. This is not a moment for Euro-fundamentalism, of whatever variety. Labour is clearly right to insist that any decision will be taken on the basis of a hard-headed assessment of British economic interests – and to have that decision ratified by the people.

But the need for a new vision for Europe goes beyond the arguments about economic and monetary union, crucial though these are. Half a century on from its post-war origins, the European Union has to be able to give a convincing account to a new generation of what it is *for*. It is not helped in this by its long subterfuge of advancing to political goals by economic means. It is time for some full-frontalism. Much of the confusion on Europe derives from uncertainty about what it is for and where it is going. The weary metaphors of missed trains and late arrivals presume a clarity about journeys and destinations that does not exist. People rightly want to know more about where they are being asked to go before they will confidently buy a ticket to ride. Eurospeak about 'ever closer union' merely increases the uncertainty and clarifies nothing.

It is crucial that Britain should have a government that can contribute positively to the restatement of European purpose and to the reform of its institutions. The Conservatives have proved beyond all doubt that they are unable to perform this role, for it requires a coherence of approach and unity of purpose that they conspicuously lack. To be *in* Europe but not *of* Europe is to be consigned to the margin. It is because Labour is committed to the European project that it can press a radical British agenda without being regarded as a mere spoiler. This is true of monetary union and the single currency, but it is also true of all the other fundamental issues that will define and shape the nature of the European enterprise in the years immediately ahead. There is the need to produce a clear constitution for Europe from the assorted confusions that presently exist. In doing so, there is the urgent need to inject more openness, democracy and legitimacy into European institutions, with an enhanced role for national parliaments. There is the need for imaginative thinking about the character of the inevitably more variegated and differentiated Europe that will come from enlargement and the ways in which some countries might develop a closer collaboration (for example, in defence and security) within a framework that is permissive rather than mandatory. The functions and procedures of a 'core' Europe need to be clearly identified and distinguished from supernumerary ones.

But in doing all of this, the overarching need is to renew a faded European vision. This means being both realistic and imaginative at the same time; realistic about the limitations of the European project and imaginative about its opportunities. It will not and should not replace the nation state as the main locus for democratic choice and routine identity, but it does enable nations to achieve together what they are less able to achieve separately. It would be useful if every EU initiative and directive had to carry a statement of the way in which it complied with this enabling criterion. The single-market programme (still in need of completion) clearly fits the bill, but so does much else. Environmental protection demands cross-national action and other areas benefit from it. Europe is a big player on issues, from world trade to human rights and development, in a way that a single medium-sized European state can never be. 'What's Europe's telephone number?' asked former US Secretary of State Henry Kissinger. And within Europe itself a jointly rising tide can succeed in lifting all boats, expressing and diffusing what is best in the European tradition of citizenship. Building the European Convention on Human Rights into the EU treaty would be a proper and popular example of this; just as an imaginative initiative to twin schools across Europe would do more for 'ever closer union' than a string of new directives.

This approach meshes with Labour's attitude to political reform at home. While the Conservative right-wing Europhobes like to proclaim their defence of the 'sovereignty' of Parliament against the usurpers of Brussels, they have been happy to watch Parliament rendered supine by the executive. Running up the flag of 'subsidiarity' in their fight with Europe, they have colluded in the attack on local government in Britain and display an unbending centralism in relation to claims for devolved power. A further, if different, irony is that their current denunciation of the effects of a European monetarism is matched only by their previous enthusiasm for its domestic version. Instead of indulging in meaningless mumbo-jumbo about sovereignty, the sensible approach is to ensure that government is conducted at the most appropriate level, which should be as close to the people as is efficiently possible. This is the case for seeking to pass power down below the level of the nation state; but it is also the case for doing some things above the level of the nation state. The nation state remains pivotal, contrary to what is sometimes claimed, but it does not exclude the need for government at other levels too.

If we can only throw off the kind of neurosis that has made us such ineffective Europeans in recent times, we can glimpse the opportunities that we now have to exercise some real influence for good in the world. The English language makes us an invaluable bridge between Europe, North America and the wider world, with enormous commercial advantages. Our cultural industries supply the world and, from fashion to pop, we are where it is at. In becoming strong again in Europe, we gain new international influence too. The United Nations needs to be made more effective, the global environmental agenda pursued with new vigour, arms exports controlled and world disarmament pursued, human rights and development made central to international policy-making: on all these issues Labour in government can provide a new impetus. We have turned in upon ourselves for too long. Now is the moment to start reaching out again.

TEN

A Civic Vision

Something is happening in Britain. There is the quietly insistent demand from the parents of Dunblane for a gun-free society. There is the powerful call for civic renewal from Frances Lawrence, whose headteacher husband was knifed to death by a teenage gang outside his school. There is, above all, the response to such voices from a public alarmed at what they see happening to their society and hungry for effective remedies. For the dramatic events connect with the daily experience of people in every street and in every community across the land, not in outrages of such singular awfulness but in a corrosive process of social insecurity. The common thread is that we have become less of a community and want to become more of a community. Behind all the promises and pledges of a general election, this is where the fundamental issue is to be found.

It is also where the indictment of this long period of Conservative rule is most stark. The composite image of the post-1992 years has its own unappealing features – from Black Wednesday to VAT on fuel, Cedric Brown to Neil Hamilton, privatization bonanzas for consultants to managerial mania in the NHS, the Great Tax Lie to the great recession, BSE to Nolan, cash-for-questions to arms-to-Iraq – but behind this record of incompetence and duplicity there lies the deeper disaster of a society being marched remorselessly in the wrong direction on the basis of a deranged ideological compass. Social, economic and technological change unsettles and challenges all societies, but what is distinctive about Britain is that it has been ruled for nearly a generation by a party in the grip of an ideology which trumpets individualism and disparages the framework of social responsibility without which individual lives soon lose their meaning and security. There was nothing inevitable about the surge in poverty and inequality, or the development of an excluded underclass, or the rising tide of insecurity: these are the consequences of political choices and decisions that were made. After the sowing comes the reaping.

Even now, despite all the rhetorical huffing and puffing from Conservative politicians in response to a public mood that they can no longer ignore, it is clear that nothing has really changed and the lessons have still not been learned. A few months ago John Major delivered a lecture that was billed as his big vision for the future (indeed, he even described it as his 'moral' vision) and it is worth recalling what he said. He identified the central Conservative task as the 'shrinking' of the state and proclaimed his 'conviction that the state should progressively disengage and do less' (*The Times*, 19 September 1996). It is often difficult to know whether Mr Major really believes what he says or whether the need to out-Redwood the Right requires such pronouncements, but whatever the reason it leaves no doubt about the direction in which the new Conservative Party has set its face. The response to a surfeit of market individualism is to be more market individualism. The demand for civic renewal is to be answered with a further repudiation of civic institutions. The need for safer streets, better schools, improved health care, secure retirement and all the other ingredients of a civilized society is met by an ambition to disengage from the collective provision that is, for most people, their prerequisite. This is as absurd as responding to a house fire by calling for a reduction in the supply of hose-pipes.

But there is no excuse now for people not knowing what the Conservatives want to do with this society. Far from altering the course they have pursued since 1979, and in the face of all its manifest consequences, they proclaim their desire to travel further and faster down the same route. They know they have to try to give a little civic top dressing to their intentions, but this merely exposes the civic vacuum at the heart of New Conservatism. When the urgent demand is for the institutions through which we express our common purposes to be strengthened, the New Conservatives propose that we 'disengage' ourselves even further from the structures of community life. This goes beyond particular arguments about how we might organize the state better, invent new institutions for new purposes, or whether taxes at particular moments are too high or too low; for what is at stake here is a repudiation of the idea of public purpose itself and the means through which it can be expressed. Whatever else may be constructed on such a basis, a new civic order will certainly not be.

Yet this is surely the moment when we are called upon to make this task central to everything else we do. It is not something that can any longer simply be taken for granted, or regarded as peripheral to other concerns, for it defines the kind of society we are and what we are able to achieve. Unless we decide now to bend all our energies and imaginations to the business of nourishing a more cohesive and responsible society, the present dislocations and discontents will be merely a foretaste of what lies ahead. Yet the demands that people make of politics and politicians are essentially modest. They require only a framework of order and security, justice and opportunity, within which they can make the best of their lives and live them in their own way. Without that framework, or as it weakens, trust is dissolved and social bonds are fractured. Those who believe that society is only a market will end up turning it into one. But those who believe, so to speak, that the only job of the state is to make the trains run on time (a modest if forlorn hope) will be hit by the lumps of concrete lobbed from the bridge. The need is less for comfortable politicians to deliver moral lectures to people who are struggling to cope and more to do all we can, in a host of concrete and practical ways, to enable people to lead worthwhile lives and bring their children up in decent and supportive environments. And if we do not want to pay to do this, then we had better be prepared to pay the price for not doing it.

We face the paradox of a society in which old constraints have been cast off, new freedoms and opportunities discovered, but where the result is not a stronger society but a weaker one. We can surf on our computer screens to every corner of the globe but we are more anxious about walking down our own street. There is no refuge in a bogus nostalgia. New freedoms (especially for women) have been genuinely liberating. The throwing off of old deferences and oppressions is pure gain. Some versions of community can be stifling and excluding. The question now is not whether we can reclaim what has been lost, something impossible even if it was desirable, but whether we can construct a new civility and community from who and what we are now. But the first question, which is also the question for this election, is whether we want to do this. Only when that decision is taken can the protracted, complex and laborious business of turning aspiration into achievement begin. The New Conservative vision of an individualized future of civic disengagement stands in sharp contrast to the New Labour civic vision of the individual-in-society within a framework of mutual responsibility. And that is the choice to be made now.

If the right choice is made, we have a better chance of becoming a happier, more contented and more successful society. 'The question is, can we be prosperous and civil too?': this central question is put by Lord Dahrendorf, who chaired the recent Commission on Wealth Creation and Social Cohesion in a Free Society. His answer, which should also be ours, is that we can. The notion that civility has to be traded for prosperity, a notion insidiously peddled by those who see social protections and securities as market obstructions, is both pernicious and misguided. We have a better chance of being both prosperous and civil if we regard these not as warring alternatives but as complementary ingredients of a good society. Balances always have to be reviewed and renegotiated of course, and defence of the status quo should never be confused with radicalism, but we should not allow ourselves to be sold false alternatives. For example, if people are called upon to adapt to more flexible working lives, they are better able to do this if there are underpinning structures of economic and social security in place. Not only is this right, but it also makes sense.

Even the yardsticks we conventionally employ to measure what is happening to our society need revision. It is a strange kind of prosperity that does not have civility built into it. Yet we measure progress in terms of GDP growth without paying equivalent attention to other measures of social health. The disjuncture between politicians' language and ordinary language reflects this. If we had a Quality of Life Index, an annual audit of our social health, we would want to measure whether the streets were safer, schools better, jobs more plentiful, health improved, poverty diminished, environment cleaner, families stronger and all the other indices of a well-functioning society. In turn, this would define an agenda for action. It might also encourage a break from the tunnel vision of a narrow departmentalism in government that makes it difficult to get a sustained hold on issues that do not sit in tidy ministerial categories.

But it requires a civic vision to be able to frame a civic agenda of this kind. And that is what has been missing. If there is no agreement on what a good society is, or a rejection even of the concept of a good society, then it is scarcely surprising that we have trouble in making progress towards it. Unless we believe in community, as a cohesive and inclusive network of mutual obligations and shared responsibilities, we shall never build such a community. Instead we shall have to live with the consequences of not building one, as we are doing now. But there should be no illusions about what Labour is offering. Far from being some kind of sepia-tinged, warm-glow soft option, it demands moral and intellectual toughness of a high order. It demands much of the state, because it has inescapable obligations to enable people to achieve collectively what they cannot achieve individually, but it demands much of individuals too. The attempt to rebalance rights and responsibilities in a way that cultivates civic virtue will no doubt prove unsettling to some, but so it should.

It will confront a culture that has been nourished over a long period, and from several directions, by a creed of possessive individualism. The consequences of this may have turned sour, but its roots have nevertheless gone deep. It is significant that even the author of a recent report from the Office of National Statistics on the erosion of traditional family structures (more than one divorce for every two marriages in 1994, 34 per cent of babies born last year to unmarried women against 7 per cent thirty years earlier, 23 per cent of families with dependent children headed by a lone parent in 1994 compared with 8 per cent in 1971) can offer in explanation only 'the growth of individualism or the

108

increasing exercise of choice' (*Population Trends* 85, 1996). It is impossible to be neutral or indifferent about this. Strong families make strong societies. Parenting is the most important activity that most of us will be required to undertake. Family breakdown can be measured by the children now entering school without basic social skills or elementary disciplines. We are paying a terrible price for the application of a choice-based individualism to the business of being a parent. In this matter, as in others, the community has an obligation to do all it can to put in place the securities and supports upon which stable families can be founded and working and family lives reconciled (for women *and* men); but this will only be successful if there is a reciprocal obligation upon individuals to regard children as something more than disposable assets or liabilities.

So this election is about fundamentals. From health to welfare, jobs to education, crime to the constitution, Labour offers an approach sharply different from that of the Conservatives. In its specific pledges it has shown, in costed detail, how its priorities would reflect this different approach. But the real difference is the fundamental one. It is the choice between more community or less, responsibility or irresponsibility, mutuality or individualism. For it is this choice that will shape every policy that is made, decision that is taken and institution that is developed. Above all, it will determine the kind of society we live in as we enter a new century and a new millennium. It is a choice of direction and of values. There are no magic levers to be pulled or buttons to be pressed. In some respects it is a civic agenda still in the making. It is a project for the long haul not for the quick burst. But it is what this election is about.

The public mood for change is evident. For many people it will be enough to get rid of a tired and discredited Government. When a party has been in power for so long that it thinks it owns the system, substituting the public interest with its own, it is time for it to go. In a political system with few formal checks and balances, depending on regular political change to refresh and restrain its operation, a prolonged period of single-party rule is likely to be corrupting. And so it has proved. The words used by Peter Thurnham, MP, when he resigned from the Conservative Party recently – 'I can no longer support a Government which has so lost touch with basic values of decency that they have forfeited the trust and respect of the British people' – will surely come to be seen as the epitaph of a regime. But this election offers more, even, than the opportunity for the country to rid itself of such a government. For what New Labour now offers is the chance for durable renewal.

A new progressive consensus and a new civic agenda is in the making. It is a moment of quite exceptional opportunity, capable of framing the politics of the next generation. Out of the exhausted ruins of the Conservative years, a new politics is being born. It is a time for radicals with imagination. The challenges and the prizes are there for all to see. Combining a market economy with social responsibility, restating the commitment to full employment, constructing new securities for a changing society, reinventing public service, strengthening neighbourhoods and communities, rebalancing rights and duties, transforming education, renewing democracy, becoming an effective player in Europe, all this – and more – defines the agenda of the period ahead. It is an agenda requiring values and vision, and a willingness to think and behave like a community, but it is an agenda for a world that has put the old sterile ideological divides behind it.

There is nothing austere about it either. It offers the prospect of a new civic culture, vital and expansive, bubbling with energy and imagination. A constituent wrote recently with the suggestion that national lottery tickets should, every quarter or so, carry vouchers for entry to concerts and theatres. And why not? Let's hope that a Department for Good Ideas (my idea) in a Labour Government will receive and generate lots of such suggestions. A responsible society takes culture and fun seriously too. We need exuberant public spaces and a vibrant popular culture. Privatization of culture and technology divides and impoverishes. Instead of culture-rich and culture-poor, information-rich and information-poor, we now have the means within our grasp as never before to universalize access and excellence. It is a genuinely exciting moment, if we choose to make it so.

And elections allow us to make such choices. By themselves, of course, they change little. On the Friday morning after the Thursday of a general election the world is still the same place and we are still the same people. But a new direction has nevertheless been chosen. This is the 3D election: dynamism, decency and democracy define the choice that New Labour is offering. In combination they open up a different kind of politics. Economic dynamism is the condition for competitive success; social decency makes a dynamic economy worth living in; and democracy is a politics for grown-ups that enables us to shape our society. This is the combination of ingredients where the politics of the future is to be found. We stand on the eve of a new progressive era, capable of matching or surpassing the great eras of the past. It requires only that we should recognize the moment and contribute to the opportunity. It's up to us.